Politics in a Religious World

POLITICS IN A RELIGIOUS WORLD

Building a Religiously Literate U.S. Foreign Policy

by
Eric Patterson

continuum

2011

Continuum International Publishing Group
80 Maiden Lane, New York, NY 10038
The Tower Building, 11 York Road, London SE1 7NX

www.continuumbooks.com

Library of Congress Cataloging-in-Publication Data
Patterson, Eric, 1971–
Politics in a religious world: building a religiously literate U.S. foreign
policy / Eric Patterson.
    p. cm.
Includes bibliographical references and index.
ISBN-13: 978-1-4411-5437-8 (hardcover: alk. paper)
ISBN-10: 1-4411-5437-X (hardcover: alk. paper)
ISBN-13: 978-1-4411-0865-4 (pbk.: alk. paper)
ISBN-10: 1-4411-0865-3 (pbk.: alk. paper) 1. United States–Foreign relations.
2. Religion and international relations. I. Title.

JZ1480.P375 2011
327.73–dc23

2011018855

ISBN   978-1-4411-0865-4 (PB)
        978-1-4411-5437-8 (HB)

Typeset by Newgen Imaging Systems Pvt Ltd, Chennai, India
Printed and bound in the United States of America

For my children,
Spencer William and Jane Margaret

Those who say religion has nothing to do with politics
do not know what religion is. — Mohandas Gandhi

Contents

Preface

In the aftermath of 9/11 I have heard countless pundits, scholars, and government officials claim, "It has nothing to do with religion." What is "It?" They are talking about a conglomerate of related issues and their intersection with religion: the attacks on the World Trade Center and Pentagon; subsequent terrorist attacks on Bali, Madrid, and London; contemporary suicide terrorism in general; the civil wars of Sudan, Somalia, and Afghanistan as well as mass violence in Iraq, Pakistan, and elsewhere; the armed response of the West to al Qaeda, its affiliates, and its admirers; the rise of Islamist politics, and decline of secular "Arab" nationalism, from the Iranian Revolution through the evolution of Turkey's ruling AKP; and the challenge of religious mobilization to the status quo in Egypt, the Palestinian Territories, Iraq, Tunisia, Yemen, and across the greater Muslim world.

In short, the "It" in the room is actually religion itself. More specifically, it is the connection between religion and violence—especially in the Middle East and Central Asia—that has the West covering its ears, eyes, and mouth. Why are political leaders so determined to call religiously informed violence something else? There are at least two distinct, and quite rational, reasons. The first is that should a Western leader, for instance a U.S. president, ever say, "We understand that a major part of contemporary conflict is the role of some forms of Islam in justifying and perpetrating the violence…" then he has acknowledged a fundamental clash of civilizations and publicly accepted what al Qaeda and other groups have been saying all along: one billion Muslims are your sworn enemy and at war with you. Of course, it is simply not true that one billion Muslims worldwide are at war with the United States, but even if 3–15 percent (depending on the survey one looks at) say that violence, including suicide bombing of civilians, is appropriate against the United States, then we are talking about millions of people who are "at war."

In short, one reason for the United States to be cautious about discussing "It" is the fear that it can become a self-fulfilling prophecy: that by acknowledging the religiously informed narratives that support violence those millions will become hundreds of millions locked in the new Cold War of the twenty-first century. And that Cold War, as evidenced on the battlefields of Iraq and Afghanistan but even more troubling in the subways of London, the trains of France, and the airports of the United States, may not be so very "cold."

I suggested that there are two reasons why senior Western leaders and thought leaders want to aver, "It has nothing to do with religion." One of the reasons has to do with what this book calls the "secularist bias" of Western foreign policies. By "secularist" I mean a disciplined intellectual choice to eschew religious and cultural factors in most cases and apply a strictly blind eye to religious factors in global affairs today. This is a "bias" because it is a choice: a decision to focus on economics, geography, natural resources, armaments, political systems, and development while excluding the religious ideas and identities that permeate most societies worldwide.

Thus, a foreign policy expert might say, "It has nothing to do with religion," not because he fears offending the Muslim world, but because he truly believes that religious phenomena are superstition, mass opiates, or ephemera that mask the "root causes" of the political turmoil within Muslim societies as well as between the West and parts of the Muslim world. For this line of thinking, it is lack of political "space," the frustrations of the middle class, the lack of jobs for college graduates, and the like that is causing the killing in Kashmir, Kandahar, and Kirkuk. This line of thinking, called secularization theory in sociology and modernization theory in political science, assumes that as societies modernize, they also become more rational, materialistic, consumerist, and ultimately, non-religious—in short, "secular." Modernization theories point to the trajectory of the West, especially Western Europe, as increasingly secular as the social welfare state expanded and citizens' material well-being advanced. The secularist bias is a materialist bias.

The problem with disregarding the "It" has many facets, described in this book. Three of the biggest are: (1) it makes it impossible to take our interlocutors at face value, (2) it fails to see all the positive intersections between religion and society, and thus (3) it makes it impossible for the United States to have a savvy, engaged, and sophisticated approach to foreign policy across government agencies. More specifically, if our friends, enemies, and the un-decided of Bosnia or Kenya or the Philippines say, "Religion is critical to our understanding of ourselves as individuals, in defining our collectives, and in understanding the basis for law and morality," we should take them very seriously. At the least, we should examine to see whether or not this is true, and if it is, then take such factors into account in our engagement. At present, our government, as an institution, does this very poorly.

Second, this approach fails to see all of the positive contributions, and possible allies, among religious people and religious groups. Yes, al Qaeda is inspired by Islam but so are Islamic Relief and the Aga Khan Foundation and hundreds of other groups working on behalf of the poor, in support of the rule of law, and against corruption and violence. Muhammad Yunus, Nobel Prize winner for his micro-credit work in Bangladesh, specifically cites Islam as a motivating force.

A religiously illiterate foreign policy can be myopic, naïve, and at times, offensive. I have experienced this secularist bias first-hand, as well as the possibilities of adding religious factors to our experience and analysis. I had the good fortune to spend 2 years at the State Department as a visiting scholar, working with some of the savviest, most intelligent people I have ever worked with. But, we routinely made mistakes with regards to religious sensitivities that are hard to assess the impact of. For instance, we took a team to visit the Afghan government and NGOs, but arrived during the end of Ramadan and wasted a couple of work days as no one was available. A year later a colleague handed around a box of donuts when we had a visiting delegation of Afghans at our U.S. office, despite the fact that Ramadan was in full swing. While in Kenya, a colleague kindly took me to visit a nature preserve for elephants and giraffes. As it was Sunday, ours was the only car to be seen heading in the direction of our destination, but thousands of Kenyans were walking the same road in precisely the opposite direction, headed to church. Perhaps we should have followed them (it was early 2007) and we would have had some sense about how religious identity would become a lever for violence in that year's presidential elections.

Despite the American taboo to not discuss "religion or politics" in polite conversation (which we routinely violate when it comes to politics), people from around the world not only often self-identify as a member of a religious community ("I am a Saudi Muslim"), but they are often curious about our own faith traditions. I recall sitting in a ramshackle café in Angola's Cabinda province with a small team from the United States and several Angolan officers. With only one translator for ten people at the table, language was difficult (the Angolans spoke Portuguese, some Russian, and bits of French and Spanish while the Americans spoke English, bits of Russian, and French and Spanish). I was far removed from the translator, so I was trying to get by in my weak Spanish, English, and gesticulations to an Angolan officer working just as hard with his Portuguese, even weaker Spanish, and hand motions. However, he noted that only he and I were drinking soda; everyone else was drinking beer. He patted his chest and said, "Baptist," and then pointed questioningly to me. I didn't try to dodge the question as a church-state violation or bother with definitions of "evangelical," the fact that the United States has 54 different Baptist denominations, or that I had grown up in a different evangelical denomination but was now attending a Baptist church. I simply smiled and answered, "Baptist." We got along very well after that.

On that same trip to Angola I was surprised, upon arrival, to see a massive Pentecostal temple in the heart of Luanda. The church was affiliated with Brazil's Universal Church of the Reign of God and is perhaps the most rapidly growing denomination within the most rapidly growing faith tradition—Pentecostal Protestantism—in the world. However, none of my American colleagues at the embassy seemed to know much about the Universal Church, despite the fact that we saw its emblem painted on dozens of shanty churches every day that we were out and about. Here is a major, rapidly growing social force in the Lusophone world, but it was off the radar screen because Angola is a "Catholic" country ruled by a Cold War-relic regime previously allied with the Soviets. I doubt that the preparation, training, and experience of other organs of the U.S. foreign policy establishment such as the intelligence community, the military, and the development and banking sectors, is much different. In fact, from my own experience as an officer in the military reserves, I have observed virtually no systematic training in the mandatory officer core curriculum regarding religion and culture.

Of course, there are positive examples of diplomats, aid workers, and military professionals who do take into account religious factors when engaging foreign publics abroad: I try to tell many of these stories in the chapters that follow. A past U.S. ambassador to Nigeria became a culture champion of Nigerian artifacts, supporting a project to digitize ancient Islamic manuscripts held in tiny village mosques in the arid north, thus making the documents available to Muslims everywhere and preserving them, digitally, for the future. This book tells the story of an apartheid-era U.S. ambassador to South Africa who attended church—both black and white congregations—and met, publicly and privately, with senior religious leaders because they were critical social voices that could lead change in the country. Although religion was not part of the calculus in the early days of the war in Iraq, the American military had to take notice when local sheikhs brought their imams to meetings, and in some cases commanders invited their chaplains to attend in a show of courtesy and reciprocity. Development experts have long known in the field that faith-based actors are key providers of services and thus partners for U.S. development activities on behalf of the most vulnerable.

This book was written with many personal experiences in mind, where religious factors played a role, where they were purposely disregarded, and where they were not even noticed. However, the book simply would not be possible without the scholarship, thinking, and debate of others. When I began work on this project, there was a single new, major report on the nexus of religious factors and U.S. foreign policy, the Center for Strategic and International Studies' *Mixed Blessings*. However, in the past year four other think tank-style reports, all discussed later in this book, were released in Washington, D.C. All of them call for an investment in knowledge resources and religious literacy by the U.S. foreign policy establishment. The most important of these, the report of the Chicago Council on Global Affairs' Task Force on Religion and U.S. Foreign Policy, is titled *Engaging Religious Communities Abroad: A New Imperative for U.S. Foreign Policy*. I was fortunate to serve, and learn, as the Project Consultant for that work and I am particularly grateful to Rachel Bronson, Vice President of the Chicago Council, for supporting this book. Indeed, much of the content in the second half of this book was developed in background papers for Task Force members and thus there are many clear parallels between the book and the Task Force report. This book also benefits from the input of Chicago Council Task Force members, notably Thomas Wright, Scott Appleby, Richard Cizik, Douglas Johnston, and Berkley Center colleagues Thomas F. Farr, Thomas Banchoff, José Casanova, Katherine Marshall, and Michael Kessler.

There are many others whose contributions, usually in print, were of great help in provoking my thinking, providing evidence, and challenging my assumptions. My research assistants, Caryl Tuma, Joseph Shamalta, Vanessa Francis, Jonathan Barsness, Ilan Cooper, and particularly Elizabeth Royall were helpful in the research and manuscript preparation. Finally, I express deep appreciation for the support of the greatest champion I know, my wife, Mary. This book is dedicated to our children, Spencer and Jane.

Note: The cover image on the front cover reminds me of Clausewitz's dictum, "War is politics by other means." The photo reflects the ambiguities of U.S. foreign policy, such as a tiny State Department dwarfed in its foreign diplomacy role by our massive Department of Defense. To me, the soldier is clearly guarding the mosque and the citizens in the vicinity, but others may have a different reaction to the image. On the one hand, the United States has saved Muslim lives in the Balkans, Indonesia, Iraq, and elsewhere, but counter-narratives argue that U.S. policies are designed to weaken the role of faith generally, and Islam specifically, on the world stage. These tensions are one theme of this book.

CHAPTER 1

Politics in a Religious World

On January 5, 2011 Malik Mumtaz Hussein Qadri was cheered by thousands and showered with rose petals when he entered a government building in Islamabad. Students, clerics, lawyers, and average citizens proclaimed that he was a national hero and a champion of Islam. According to the BBC, upon leaving the court Qadri was garlanded with flowers by a supporter and rallied the crowd by shouting, "Allah Akbar!" (God is Great!).[1] On the same day, in Lahore, Pakistani Prime Minister Yousuf Raza Gilani led thousands of mourners at the funeral of Punjab Governor Salman Taseer, a senior member of the Pakistan People's Party. Taseer was remembered as a public servant, supporter of democracy, and liberal reformer. Taseer had been assassinated a few days earlier by one of his retinue of police bodyguards.

It was Qadri who murdered Taseer. Why? And is this assassination relevant to U.S. foreign policy?

Qadri is transparent in providing a rationale for the killing: Taseer's support for an apostate made him a wicked blasphemer. The story goes back over a year, to charges that a Christian Pakistani woman, Asia Bibi, had blasphemed the Prophet Muhammad. Bibi, an illiterate mother of five, was imprisoned and sentenced to death by hanging under Pakistan's national blasphemy law. The local imam in her town of Ittan Wali says that he cried for joy at the verdict and he is certain that "justice" will be done: "If the law punishes someone for blasphemy, and that person is pardoned, then we will also take the law in our hands."[2]

Governor Taseer had taken a vocal, public stand against the blasphemy law, making many enemies in Pakistan. It would be inaccurate to suggest that only a tiny minority of Pakistanis support such a law. The 2007 Pew Global Attitudes Survey found that 78 percent of Pakistanis strongly support the death penalty for blasphemy.[3] In this context, many social and religious leaders have justified not only the death penalty for Asia Bibi, but also the extrajudicial execution of Governor Taseer. He received numerous death threats since bringing the case of Asia Bibi to national attention.

Jamaat-e-Ahl-e-Sunnat Pakistan, a religious political party, issued the following statement: "No Muslim should attend the funeral or even try to pray for Salman Taseer or even express any kind of regret or sympathy over the incident." The Pakistani Taliban's Ehsanullah Ehsan challenged religious leaders to remian steadfast in support of the blasphemy law and said that those who supported or prayed for Taseer were blasphemers as well.[4]

Does any of this matter to the United States? Does the case against Asia Bibi have any connection to U.S. foreign policy? Does the assassination of Governor Taseer, and the mixed response of the Pakistani people, portend anything for the United States? Or, is this a local matter, half the world away? Is it simply a vestige of unfinished modernity that will only find a solution when Pakistanis address the "root causes" of social dissatisfaction and create a vibrant economy within the democratic rule of law?

Whether the United States likes it or not, the assassination of Governor Taseer, the case of Asia Bibi, the treachery of Qadri and its religious justifications, and the contending forces on multiple sides of the issue all have direct connections to and consequences for U.S. foreign policy. The United States is fighting a war in neighboring Afghanistan and an undeclared war against al Qaeda and Taliban militants in Pakistan's ungoverned border regions. The primary supply chain for U.S. forces in Afghanistan is through Pakistan. The United States cannot come to terms with Pakistan's quixotic blend of Muslim nationalism and national paranoia without understanding the nexus of national identity, religious identification, and the self-reinforcing existential threat of Hindu India. Pakistan is a nuclear power with an unstable government, dangerous ethnic cleavages, and a state of war on both of its major borders. It is headquarters to not only al Qaeda and at least two distinct forms of Taliban, but also to dozens of other religiously inspired extremist groups, such as Lashkar-e-Taiba (responsible for the 2008 Mumbai attacks), Sipah-e-Sahaba, Jaish-e-Muhammad, and the Harakat ul-Mujahadeen.[5] Many of these groups have direct ties to elements of the military or Pakistan's Inter-Services Intelligence (ISI) directorate that date to the 1980s.

With a population of 184 million, Pakistan is a critical player in South Central Asia; its trials and tribulations have regional significance. Pakistan's economic development challenges are immense, and the United States has spent billions not just on modernizing elements of Pakistan's military but also in trying to provide humanitarian relief. Pakistan's poor human rights record and its abuse of individual liberties, such as religious freedom, routinely make it a target of U.S. human rights laws like the 1998 International Religious Freedom Act. In sum, it is difficult to think that the case of Asia Bibi was an isolated instance in Pakistan—it is simply one example of thousands of systematic persecution of individuals, be they Christians, Ahmadis, Sikhs, or others. And this nuclear-armed, unstable, violent, and dangerous country is home to both key U.S. supporters and to the United States' bitterest enemies.

One could not make sense of any of this without at least an appreciation that religious factors matter in Pakistan and South Asia. Wise U.S. foreign policy cannot be developed without some comprehension of the religious currents in that society; however, understanding religious issues has not been a key part of U.S. foreign policy. Later chapters will demonstrate that while a secularist bias is pervasive in U.S. foreign policy for a variety of reasons, it means that the way we train our foreign policy experts and the way we deal with foreign countries is often characterized by a "missing dimension": religion.[6]

U.S. Foreign Policy and the Global Resurgence of Religion

American policy practitioners are struggling to respond to what political scientist Scott Thomas has called the "global resurgence of religion and the transformation of international affairs."[7] The events of the last 15 years—from Bosnian massacres to the productive role of religion-oriented political parties in Indonesia—have made clear that religion is a major factor in global affairs, and that the United States requires a much deeper and more nuanced understanding of religion. Many across the U.S. foreign policy establishment accept this, but question exactly how and when it matters and what to do about it.

This newfound interest in religion comes after a series of events beginning with the 1979 Iranian Revolution that brought religion to the fore. More recently, a series of blunders in U.S. foreign policy resulted from disregarding the religious context in which the United States was operating, making clear that a far more nuanced understanding of religion was required if the United States was to succeed in this changing international environment.

At the end of the Cold War, some began to see new ideational forces emerging that would define global affairs in the years to come. In 1992 Benjamin Barber predicted increased conflict that he called Jihad ("tribalism," aggressive religiosity) versus McWorld (globalization, secularism).[8] At the same time, in two influential books Samuel Huntington detailed an international "third wave of democracy" that was largely fueled by liberalization in the Catholic Church and the fall of authoritarian regimes; and separately, that religious revival in other regions, caused by economic modernization and social change, would increasingly stir up violence along "civilizational" fractures. Huntington defined "civilization" as a cross-nationally shared religion and culture, and his controversial thesis seemed to explain ethnoreligious violence in places like Bosnia, Sri Lanka, and Kashmir.[9] To the observer of the 1990s, religious elements were intertwined with political mobilization, identity, war, and peace. The Islamic Refah Party won an impressive plurality in Turkey; surprisingly large and bold peace marches led by Cambodia's Buddhist primate helped support reconciliation efforts in that country; Latin American democracies began to consolidate with the support of the Catholic Church; religious actors promoted conflict and peace in northern Ireland and Cyprus; and Algeria and Egypt, among others, struggled to manage the return of militant "Afghan Arabs."

However in the early- and mid-1990s there was almost no writing, either academic or policy-focused, that focused directly on the nexus of religion and U.S. foreign policy. The one, critical exception was Douglas Johnston and Cynthia Sampson's *Religion, the Missing Dimension of Statecraft*. The book argued that contrary to its interests, U.S. foreign policy is blind to religious factors in international affairs. *The Missing Dimension* cited many then-recent encounters where the United States was blithely unaware of the religious dimension, including the religious mobilization of Ayatollah Khomeini in Iran, the motives of the pro-democracy religious Left in Latin America, and the religious basis for factionalization in Lebanon's civil war. Unfortunately, as *The Missing Dimension* was published at a moment when foreign policy thinking was still tied to Cold War constructs, its message fell on deaf ears in policy circles. The quick pace of new conflicts that demanded the attention of policymakers (e.g., Haiti, Somalia, Rwanda), also seemed different enough from the cases that the book identified to allow its key messages to be overlooked.

Although analysts interested in better understanding and incorporating religion were operating largely independently and often in the margins in the late 1990s, they were joined by greater numbers after the September 11 attack on the United States. Eighteen months later, when the United States invaded Iraq—with apparently little appreciation for the religious, historical, and cultural context it was entering, among other shortcomings—events on the ground demanded a dramatic rethink of the role of religion and its importance to U.S. foreign policy.

Without fully grappling with new realities of international affairs, including the global resurgence of religion, U.S. decision makers will approach foreign policy in the twenty-first century with one hand tied behind their backs. This is not to say that Americans should trade a secularist bias for a religionist bias: this book is not asserting that religion is everything. But, religion is often important to other cultures and political systems and therefore a certain religious literacy should be incorporated into U.S. policy. More specifically, in approaching a highly religious world, U.S. foreign policy should take religion and religious actors seriously on their own terms, invest in a basic level of religious literacy for some of its foreign policy experts, and draw upon the rich religious capital of its citizenry.

It is doubtful that U.S. foreign policy will hyper-fixate on religious phenomena. What is more likely, and this book cautions against, is considering religious dynamics to always be "the problem." There is a tendency, particularly since al Qaeda declared war on the United States in the 1990s using religious justifications, to consider religion only as a driver of conflict, divisive, the cause of parochialism, superstition, unjust hierarchies, and war. This is unfair and unwise in at least two ways. First, such an approach narrowly circumscribes religious variables as "subjects" for micro-study, usually without deeper understandings of culture and wider analyses of cross- and transnational trends. Second, the "religion as problem" thesis neglects the many positive roles and effects of religious multidimensionality in world affairs: humanitarian assistance, education, peacemaking and peacebuilding, moral conscience, and Track 2 diplomacy, to name a few. In short, U.S. foreign policy should instead recognize a "religion as opportunity" moment in world affairs, during which humility, religious awareness, and a willingness to learn and collaborate promise new partnerships, better understanding, and the advancement of American ideals and interests.

Religious Trends in International Affairs

The impact of religion on world affairs may be the most important feature of international life since the end of the Cold War. It is a reawakening of people to spiritual and associational life on every inhabited continent, wherein hundreds of millions of people practice their faith as individuals as well as in communities. It is also a reawakening of scholars to the diverse religious dynamics possible in world affairs. Simply put, the way that faith operates differs dramatically in the lives of individuals, families, and nations; and American policy practitioners would be shortsighted to overlook its important influence on domestic, international, and transnational politics.

Religion is an organized, shared set of beliefs and practices founded on reverence for a supernatural power(s) or in the teachings of a spiritual leader.[10] Five general trends characterize this global resurgence of religion and possible intersections with U.S. foreign policy: (1) individual religiosity is rising the world over; (2) public expression of religion by individuals and groups worldwide matters more in political discourse; (3) states are no longer the sole legitimate centers of authority and authenticity, nor are they always the most reliable providers of vital services; (4) religious actors, identities, and ideas are vigorously transnational; and (5) whether at the individual or collective level, religious impulses can transcend what scholars typically define as "rational" or material interests.

Individual religiosity—religious devotion and activity—is rising the world over. Surveys indicate the following trends:

- Over the past 20 years, belief in God has risen on every inhabited continent except Western Europe. In Eastern Europe, for example, belief in God has risen 10 percent.
- The proportion of people attached to the world's four biggest religions (Christianity, Islam, Buddhism and Hinduism) rose from 67 percent in 1900 to 73 percent in 2005 and may reach 80 percent by 2050.
- Majorities of publics in key regional players report that religion is "*very* important to their life," including Indonesia, Pakistan, Nigeria, Egypt, Turkey, South Africa, India, and Brazil.
- Over 90 percent of the publics in 46 countries surveyed say that religious freedom is important to them.[11]

This vitalization is not primarily in formal religious structures, but rather in the "lived religion" of individuals and their communities.[12] "Lived religion" is defined as the concrete, everyday behaviors of religious actors and the sensibilities underlying these behaviors, as well as the dynamic expression of that religion (i.e., doctrines, heritages, texts, practices, and formal ethics) translated into daily life and collective action. In short, individual faith continues to be intertwined with culture, ethnicity, collective identity, authority, and sometimes nationalism. Scott Thomas writes,

> the global resurgence of religion is the growing saliency and persuasiveness of religion, i.e., the increasing importance of religious beliefs, practice, and discourses in persona and public life, and the growing role of religious or religiously related individuals, non-state groups, political parties, and communities, and organizations in domestic politics, and this is occurring in ways that have significant implications for international politics.[13]

What does this mean for U.S. foreign policy? It is beyond the scope of this book (or for the U.S. government) to consider all that religious and spiritual experience means in the personal lives of billions of adherents around the globe. Nonetheless, the upsurge in individual religiosity is meaningful to U.S. foreign policy is many ways. Religious people are using their worldview to frame challenges to ineffective governance, corruption, partisanship, and social programs that they believe violate their values. According to Philip Jenkins, 20 of the world's

25 largest countries have some mix of Muslims and Christians and nearly half of those "are by present outlook…ripe for conflict and persecution" in ways that could lead to all-out war.[14] Religious people appeal for assistance to, and criticize the activities of, other governments—including U.S. foreign policies—as well as international institutions and transnational NGOs. Religious people are taking action based on their understanding of the mandates of their faith in realms as diverse as philanthropy and armed resistance.

Second, the rise in individual religiosity encourages an *increase in the public expression of religion by individuals and groups worldwide.* This phenomenon, growing over the past 15 years, has been called by José Casanova the "deprivatization of religion," confounding neat separations of church and state.[15] As people become more religiously aware and active, the result is collective action informed by faith or in concert with members of broad religious networks. Such activity can take a multiplicity of forms from public acts of veneration with sociopolitical implications to local acts of charity (that may engage local political actors or ordinances) to far wider mobilizations for freedom of expression, in support of political platforms, or against social programming.

The world is witnessing a vibrant blending of religious impulses, actors, and coalitions on a host of issues in the public square. Since the Cold War's end religion has become a "dominant social medium" in many societies for dialogue and action on society and politics, in much the same way that secular Arab nationalism provided a collective action frame and political program in the 1960s.[16] An example of these trends is the peace marches led by Cambodia's Buddhist primate Maha Ghosananda in the early 1990s during a turbulent period of political transition amid seesawing violence. Ten thousand people joined him in 1993 despite threats, a belligerent Khmer Rouge, landmines, and other dangers. The *Dhammayietra* (Pilgrimage of Truth) and Ghosananda's moral leadership provided moral support to UN-sponsored elections, tacitly criticized violence among Cambodians, and inspired reconciliation efforts.[17] Indeed, to the surprise of many in the West who imagine only a passive Buddhism, religious faith motivated the Buddhist *sangha* to fight Sri Lanka's long civil war, Buddhist monks led a Saffron Revolution against the Burmese regime, and in Thailand Buddhist monks were at the forefront of rallies that led to the ouster of the prime minister.

This book is not arguing that religion is necessarily becoming politicized or that politics is becoming more religious (although both are likely true in some contexts). Rather, religious factors are no longer banished to houses of worship, if they ever were, but are increasingly infused into all facets of public life. This broadening of the public sphere to include religious actors means that our old academic constructs for studying politics (e.g., focus on government leaders, rules, economic outputs) are too simplistic to reasonably account for the much broader and deeper social and cultural phenomena inherent to society.

Religious actors compete with states as centers of legitimate authority, identity, and authenticity, and may be more reliable providers of vital services. Much has been written about the decline of states in an era of globalization. Globalization "shrinks" international society due to advances in communications, travel, and technology fueling economic, political, and ultimately cross-civilizational interdependence. Globalization's advocates also point to a widened cast of political actors, most notably the United Nations, but also including multinational corporations, international relief organizations, transnational terrorist networks, and other communities of choice.

What development experts tell us, looking from the inside out, is that governments have long been weakening. Within domestic society, actors make appeals for legitimacy based on effectiveness or ethics and have widespread authority within their communities. Religious actors in many places fit this bill: Catholic cardinals in Latin America, Anglican Archbishops in Nigeria and Kenya, Grand Ayatollah Ali Sistani among Iraq's majority Shiites. Elsewhere, Afghanistan's Taliban and Somalia's Islamic Courts Union claimed legitimacy based on practicing their faith and providing security.

U.S. government representatives with "boots on the ground" in the developing world observe this every day: they work with and alongside a host of partners, many of whom are religious, particularly in the arenas of economic development and humanitarian assistance. Often the most effective and most legitimate care providers in situations of poverty and development are those inspired by faith: hospitals, food programs, and orphanages run by community-entrenched religious orders and faith-based organizations. U.S. foreign policy needs to carefully consider how to develop respectful relations with social and transnational actors who are not government agents but have widespread legitimacy and significant followings, religious or not, in the changing international landscape.

Religious actors, identities, and ideas are vigorously transnational. Religion, exuding from personal and collective experience and motivating public expressions of faith and religiously inspired social action, has become vigorously transnational in the context of multiple centers of social and political legitimacy within state borders. Unlike ethnicity and nationalism, limited by localized geographic claims, religion can be international, even global, in its claims of shared identity and morality. This is a key feature of globalization that has been overlooked.

Religious virtuosi can be transnational in message and effect, much like televangelists, Catholic popes, and the Dalai Lama.[18] Religious actors can concentrate resources and attention on a specific global hotspot, as the 50,000-member Community of Sant'Egidio did in convening peace talks in Algeria and Mozambique. Extremist Muslim groups can fundraise across the globe, as they have done over the past decade. Transnational religious identity can call the entire Western state concept into question, as some argue the notions of "universal church" or "*ummah*" do in Christianity and Islam respectively.

This trend is occurring as the twentieth century's major secular transnational ideologies are on the wane. There was a time when claims of "The Revolution" in the form of the universal proletariat, transnational fascism, or secular Arab nationalism seemed to be the dominant intellectual competitors to key values and interests of the United States. Today those challengers have all fallen by the wayside, and much of the world is experiencing excited political debate on numerous topics—but most of those debates include transnational voices and constituencies operating within religious worldviews and across religious networks.

Religious themes can inspire collaboration, for good or ill, across state boundaries in the globalized world in ways unimagined just a decade or two ago, such as the organization of disparate terrorist cells across the Muslim world into a loose al Qaeda confederacy or the way that persecuted "house church" Christians in China—some 50 million strong today—have reached out to co-religionists in North America to plead their case for religious freedom.

Transnational religious alliances across religious divides prove more potent when they work in solidarity toward a common cause. One such cause is the rallying of national and transnational religious bodies behind the Millennium Development Goals (MDGs). Examples include the Micah Challenge (a global coalition of over 300 largely evangelical Christian organizations) and the World Council of Religions Parliament (2006) in Kyoto that provided workshops to 600 religious leaders on the MDGs. The internet is also becoming a transnational domain for religiously inspired activity against poverty. One example is Kiva, a faith-based online tool that connects donors directly with entrepreneurs in the developing world. The founder, Jessica Jackley, was inspired by a lecture by Dr. Muhammad Yunus at Stanford University, 3 years before Yunnus was awarded the Nobel Prize for the micro-credit revolution that he pioneered. Loans in Kiva's first year totaled $500,000 and $14 million the second year; by early 2011 they had given nearly $192 million in loans.[19] In short, faith-based groups both "take matters into their own hands" to fight global poverty, and directly engage the G-8, the UN, the World Bank, the IMF, and the individual governments of wealthy countries.

Finally, the transnational nature of religion is part of broader trends in globalization such as immigration, religious cross-pollination, and financial remittances. For the average person, particularly in places like the United States and Western Europe and many major urban centers worldwide, this means increasing interaction with people of different backgrounds, causing reflection (and sometimes action) on individual and collective religious identities and ideals. In other words, millions of citizens are having to reflect on relating to their new neighbor-down-the-street of a "foreign" religious faith, the interreligious dating of their teenager, the country to which their son or daughter was deployed, changes in the curricula of their local school, and the like. The scope and magnitude of this very real and very personal "glocalization" suggests a new era and unique challenges for tens of millions of average citizens worldwide.[20]

A fifth observation regarding religion is as old as faith itself: *religious faith is a potent motivator of individuals, organizations, and societies that can transcend material interests.* When religious faith is a personal, private thing then few notice this significant point. However, when giving, sacrificial faith expresses itself publicly, corporately, or violently, then it has all eyes upon it. This is true when Archbishop Desmond Tutu marched, despite death threats, against apartheid; it is equally true when a Black Widow suicide bomber leaves her family to kill others. What makes religious activity difficult for traditional social science is that it can defy the materialist assumptions of secularist models—people give their time, money, energy, and devotion in ways that transcend narrow material definitions of "self-interest." Of course, this should be no surprise, as people are often inspired by things other than wealth, but so much of political analysis focuses on material give-and-take. In short, the increase of individual and corporate religious activity in the public sphere means that new thinking about what terms like "collective security," "shared interests," and "rational behavior" means, and how religious ideas and identities create new definitions of security, interests, and rational behavior.

In sum, today's world is characterized by the salience of religious actors, ideas, and influences for individuals, collectives, states, and the international system. Religious faith is a personal matter, but religion also poses social complexities in world affairs like ethnoreligious cleansing in the Balkans, the rise and fall and rise of the Taliban, and the current reverse migration of Somalis from the suburbs of Washington, D.C., to fight for the al-Shaba'ab on the outskirts of Mogadishu. The United States needs a twenty-first century foreign policy approach that takes into account the causes and significance of these phenomena and can translate that understanding into sensible policy action by the U.S. government.

Outline of the Book

The overall purpose of this book is to argue that U.S. foreign policy must engage the world as it is, including its vibrant religiosity. For this book, foreign policy is broadly defined as the goals and activities of the U.S. government in its interactions abroad. To do so, the United States must develop a basic religious literacy in its foreign policy establishment and tap into the uniquely American reserves of religious capital in its society. However, the next two chapters discuss why U.S. foreign policy has so often failed to appreciate the religious dynamics of global affairs. Chapter 2 provides part of the answer: academic approaches to the study of international affairs, known as international relations (IR) theory, have purposely left religion out of their discussions. IR theory has had three internal "Great Debates" over the past 75 years, but in none of them were religious factors considered to be an issue by either party to the debate. The most important of these Great Debates, between "realism" and "liberalism" (or "liberal internationalism") not only structures major elements of the theoretical literature, but also much of contemporary American statecraft. Chapter 2 argues that at the nexus of IR theory and actual diplomacy a fourth Great Debate is being waged over whether or not to let religion in to the analysis. The chapter concludes by looking at examples of this debate, from the traditional IR theory work of Daniel Philpott and Elizabeth Shakman Hurd to some of the most recent statements of U.S. diplomatic and national security policy. These latter generally label religion as "the problem" or avoid the topic altogether, as in the case of the Obama Administration's 2010 National Security Strategy, which warns that "race, religion, and region" have "polarized us" in the past, but that a renewed sense of "shared interests" will lead to peace.

Chapters 3 and 4 argue that day-to-day U.S. foreign policy tends to be blind to the five religious trends and that awkward, muddling, and insensitive policies have damaged U.S. interests and security. This book calls the traditional approach to U.S. foreign policy over the last half century "secularist," meaning that it been actively biased against analysis of and engagement with the religious multidimensionality of the world. Edward Luttwak calls this bias "a learned repugnance to contend *intellectually* with all that is religion..."[21] That secularist bias characterizes the higher education offerings of political science and law, infuses the professional training of soldiers, Foreign Service officers, and aid experts, and severely hamstrings the actual practice of U.S. foreign policy when interacting with highly religious publics. Chapter 4 demonstrates that scholars need not throw the baby out with the bath water: many of the existing frameworks, such as realism and liberalism, have the internal resources within themselves to engage, reflect on, and theorize about religious phenomena—they have simply chosen not to in the past.

This book is not alone in calling for a reappraisal of U.S. foreign policy with regard to religious phenomena. In the year that this book was written, at least four think tank reports called for comparable "new thinking" in U.S. foreign policy. Indeed, there have been similar calls by senior leaders such as former Secretary of Defense Robert Gates and former Secretary of State Madeline Albright. In preparing this book the author also learned about a number of initiatives within the government to consider and act on the positive potential as well as risks associated with religious dynamics in international life, but in general such activities are ad hoc, short-term, poorly resourced, and the result of individual initiative rather than systematic, institutionalized, appropriately funded, and supported by senior management.

Chapters 5 and 6 call for a baseline of religious literacy in U.S. foreign policy. It is not that the United States needs to hire religious people into its foreign service, military, and aid agencies, but that it needs to develop a base level of religious literacy for individuals deploying on behalf of the United States to highly religious societies, be it the U.S. ambassador in Manila or a USAID employee in Mauritania. The term "religious literacy," as defined by Boston University professor Stephen Prothero, is "the ability to understand and use in one's day-to-day life the basic building blocks of religious traditions—their key terms, doctrines, symbols, sayings, characters, metaphors, and narratives."[22] For the purposes of this book, religious literacy in U.S. foreign policy is a basic awareness of the importance of religious factors in their relevant context. Chapters 5 and 6 demonstrate how religious literacy helps one understand the religious multidimensionality of many of today's conflicts as well as religiously inspired efforts for peace, like the work of Community Sant'Egidio in brokering a peace accord to end Mozambique's civil war. Chapter 6 also develops in some detail the links between religious literacy and key vectors of U.S. foreign policy: support for economic development, human rights, and the promotion of sustainable democracy.

Chapter 7 lays out four general recommendations for U.S. foreign policy and provides a number of sub-recommendations and examples for a way forward. The first recommendation is for the White House and Cabinet-level officials to publicly identify this as critical area for the national interest and clarify the appropriate domain for engaging religious factors in order to overcome bureaucratic resistance and inertia against encountering religious actors and societies in order to circumvent Establishment Clause concerns. The second and third recommendations call for expanded training and knowledge resources to be incorporated in the professional development of foreign affairs specialists, regardless of agency, in order to develop a baseline of religious literacy. In addition, a range of long-term investment is needed in this area, from human capital to research and education in American universities to building relationships with credible religious representatives of foreign societies.

Finally, Chapter 7 recommends that a broad political strategy be developed and implemented for encountering a religious world. That strategy, which could and should be quickly developed, would be multifaceted, including existing programs on religion (such as America's commitments under the 1998 International Religious Freedom Act) as well as revamped public diplomacy and interreligious dialogue, like that called for in President Obama's executive order directing collaboration between the National Security Council and his then-newly constituted Advisory Council on Faith-Based and Neighborhood Partnerships.

The book challenges the reader to consider a future where religious literacy is appropriately integrated into U.S. foreign policy, in ways analogous to the integration of economics or other disciplines, and concludes in Chapter 8 with a few examples of how religiously literate diplomacy can make for smarter foreign policy: the personal initiative of an ambassador to quietly build relationships with influential clerics in Africa; the planning and sensitivity necessary (but unrealized) to identify, understand, and partner with religious leaders in Iraq from 2003 to 2008; and excellent USAID-funded programming on democracy, human rights, health, and development around the world.

The book concludes with good news: America has a deep reservoir of religious capital, and this capital can be called upon to inform its foreign policy. More specifically, the American public is very religious by Western standards and as an immigrant nation includes vital communities of faith that can provide knowledge about faith tradition and practice for any country around the globe. The United States also has more intellectual resources in its universities and think tanks than any other Western country, and it has the experience of some of its foreign policy leaders—typically not recorded in official cables, but real nonetheless—who can provide insight to the next generation of foreign policy experts on these issues. Moreover, the United States has a cadre of faith-based organizations and unofficial Track 2 diplomats who work behind the scenes to liberate the imprisoned, enhance cross-sectarian understanding, promote security and peace, and work as trusted intermediaries "off the record" to leaders on both sides of a conflict.

For the foreseeable future the United States will pursue its interests and ideals in a world inhabited by billions of highly religious people. Its interests and ideals will be challenged in places like Pakistan, where strategic considerations regarding al Qaeda, the Taliban, nuclear weapons, and regional security are inextricably linked to the assassination of political leaders, the rise of religious martyrs, and tragic cases like that of Asia Bibi. The first step is to better understand the multidimensionality of the religious world at the beginning of the twenty-first century, but in order to do so, U.S. foreign policy must overcome its self-imposed intellectual limitations within the scholarly and professional communities.

CHAPTER 2

International Relations' Next Great Debate: Bringing Religion In

Some of the basic details of the 9/11 attacks are well-known: a group of Islamist radicals known as al Qaeda hijacked four U.S. jetliners in accordance with Osama bin Laden's fatwa against America and its allies: "We—with God's help—call on every Muslim who believes in God and wishes to be rewarded to comply with God's order to kill the Americans and plunder their money wherever and whenever they find it."[1] The hijackers, typically posing as students, took control of the passenger aircraft, ramming two of them into New York City's Twin Towers and a third into the Pentagon in Washington, D.C.; the fourth plane was brought down in the Pennsylvania countryside due to the courage of its imprisoned passengers.

What was their objective? Was it to kill some Americans? Was it to kill as many Americans as possible? Was it "shock and awe?" Was the goal a media splash and thus instant, global notoriety on behalf of their cause? Was the attack intended by modern-day nihilists to cause panic and chaos, or perhaps designed to demonstrate valor and sacrifice to the Muslim *ummah*?

Notre Dame scholar Daniel Philpott argues that the 9/11 attacks were an attack on the entire Western-inspired structure of international relations.[2] The architecture of international affairs, rooted in the 1648 Peace of Westphalia that established the notion of sovereign states and non-intervention, is premised on national governments competing and cooperating across their man-made borders via secular international law and international institutions like the UN. The principles underlying this system are decidedly Western; not simply in historical origin, but in their philosophical roots, particularly those of representative governments based on popular sovereignty, individual autonomy, and the competitive nature of Western capitalism. According to Philpott, the 9/11 attacks are a thoughtful, decisive declaration of war on the West's "Westphalian" model of international relations; al Qaeda's explicit alternative is a global caliphate inhabited by citizens united by religious faith (*ummah*) where God alone is sovereign and his will, as expressed in the Quran and hadiths, is the basis not only for criminal law but for the entire ordering of society (sharia).

Philpott's analysis is one of the few in international relations (IR) theory to approach the 9/11 attacks in formal, theoretical terms. One of the reasons that this type of analysis is rare is because religious factors have typically been explained away or excluded as irrelevant in traditional IR theory. In order to understand why this is so, this chapter is divided into two parts. The first part provides background describing the intellectual currents that led to where we are today; the second half looks specifically at fresh government documents like the U.S. National Security Strategy of 2010, which largely neglect religion in international affairs.

More specifically, the first half of the chapter demonstrates how the three so-called "Great Debates" of IR theory—as an academic discipline—largely neglected religion. Consequently U.S. foreign policy in practice, whether influenced by realism's focus on power politics between countries or liberalism's conviction that shared material and security interests can provide peace, generally ignored religious factors. The chapter also shows how a new debate, which I call the "fourth Great Debate," is over whether or not to allow religious variables into contemporary scholarly and policy analysis, and if so, whether religion is always to be considered a "problem" to be dealt with, a "tool" to be manipulated, or something else. Recent U.S. foreign policy documents, most notably the National Security Strategy and the National Intelligence Council's *Global Trends 2025*, unfortunately continue to overlook religious elements as much as possible.

International Relations' Three Great Debates

The academic discipline of IR theory is inextricably linked to reflection on and action in U.S. foreign and national security policies. In other words, the underlying theoretical assumptions that drive policymaking and define the paradigmatic understanding of global affairs directly affect the assumptions of foreign policy practitioners, such as whether it is a competitive, power politics world ("realism") or one where reasonable people should expect progressive social evolution toward peace and cooperation over time ("liberalism"). Over the past 75 years, the scholarly discipline of IR theory has been energized by three "Great Debates," all of which have ramifications for how international relations is "done" both as a scholarly enterprise (teaching, research) and in the day-to-day affairs of diplomacy. This chapter summarizes those debates, their deliberate exclusion of religious factors, and then proposes that the IR theory/foreign policy nexus is seeing a fourth "Great Debate": whether or not to systematically integrate religious phenomena into theory and practice.

The First Great Debate: Realism vs. Liberalism

Although World War I was supposed to be the "war to end all wars," it sowed the seeds for World War II. This interwar period also sowed the first Great Debate in IR theory, that between realism and liberalism. On the one hand, "liberals" or "idealists" believed that the cause of war was the anarchic system of power politics which could be rationally modified through international law (e.g., Kellogg-Briand Pact outlawing war), international institutions (e.g., League of Nations), transparency, mutually beneficial trade, and democratic reforms such as self-determination, representative government, and the rule of law in an open society (e.g., U.S. President Woodrow Wilson's Fourteen Points). Liberals, the forerunners of today's liberal internationalists, were informed by the progressive and rationalist elements then dominant in Western capitals—that peace, prosperity, and human advancement were all possible through the steady evolution of individuals and societies. Thus, liberalism spawned genres of research on economics and trade (as a mechanism for peace), collective security, constitutional architectures for domestic and international life, and global cooperation that worked in tandem with the liberal-idealist aspirations of world leaders such as Wilson, and disarmament devotees and Prime Ministers Stanley Baldwin (Tory) and Ramsey MacDonald (Labour).

E. H. Carr launched a full-scale intellectual war against liberalism, as theory and policy, with his *The Twenty Years Crisis: 1919–1939.*[3] Carr argued that the idealism of Wilson and other liberals led to an unrealistic, and dangerous, approach to foreign policy. Carr and other "realists" like Reinhold Niebuhr, George Kennan, Hans J. Morgenthau resurrected the "realist" approach to international relations associated with Thucydides, Machiavelli, Hobbes, and other thinkers, arguing that international relations is characterized by anarchy, power politics, competition among state actors, and the enduring problem of war. Indeed, realists over the next several decades focused much of their intellectual energies on understanding the causes of war: the security dilemma, power "balancing" vs. "bandwaggoning," the role of human nature (fallen and sinful or in a Darwinian struggle for survival?), hegemonic stability theory, and the like.

In sum, the contending theoretical approaches of liberalism and realism, in all their varieties, make up the first Great Debate of IR theory. This debate continues to this day, as self-proclaimed realists still contend in the pages of *Foreign Affairs* and *Foreign Policy* magazines about how best to deal with global terrorism, the wars in Central Asia, rising China, and international institutions. More importantly, from the 1930s through today, these theoretical positions have not only informed the IR and political science classroom and professorial scholarship, but also the approach and thinking of every major Western foreign policy practitioner, from the U.S. president to Canada's prime minister, to the British Foreign Secretary. However, as described in the next chapter, despite their utility these two traditions generally fail to account for or understand religious factors in theory or in practice, and thus are self-limiting in understanding the strategic context of the twenty-first century.

The Second Great Debate: Traditionalists vs. Behaviorists

Beginning sometime in the late 1950s, a second Great Debate began to overlap the first. This debate, between traditionalists on one hand and so-called behaviorists on the other, had major implications both for scholarship and for practice. The traditionalist camp was largely made up of realists and liberals who felt that the interdisciplinary nature of IR theory and its application to real-world foreign policy was not only a strength but its fundamental purpose. Traditionalists argued that the scholarly blend of political science, history, ethics, current events analysis, economics, international law, and sociology in tandem with the ebb and flow of real-world security events was the right trajectory for IR theory. In contrast, there was a move in some quarters to move the discipline of "political science" away from normative arguments, history, ethics, and other disciplines (e.g., economics) in favor of "scientific" methodologies. This latter group tends to be called behaviorists, and they were responding in part to the new techniques of survey research and mathematical modeling available for study of domestic constituencies as well as in comparative studies of societies around the world. Behaviorists were also attempting to make "political science" a science based on rigorous quantitative methods on par with math, engineering, physics and other competitors for government research dollars in the Sputnik era.

During the second Great Debate, realism and liberalism continued to dominate the arguments between foreign policy professionals and national leaders in addressing critical issues of the day: how to deal with the Soviet Union, the utility and promise of international law and organizations, the role of trade as a strategic "weapons system" or as the catalyst for peace, the significance of postcolonial transitions, what to make of deterrence theory and the nuclear arms race, and so on. However, particularly within U.S. universities, behaviorism won wide sway over what has come to be known as the subdiscipline of American Politics, as represented by its prominence within the American Political Science Association and its flagship journal, the *American Political Science Review*. The behaviorist revolution was to make census, survey, polling, and other forms of quantitative data analysis the scientific approach to the study of politics, and this largely permeates the domestic study of politics to this day. Lost in this second Great Debate between traditional realists and liberals, with their focus on the Cold War struggle against Communism and the behaviorist focus on quantitative methodologies, were the effects of religious factors in international relations as a theoretical enterprise and in its relationship to foreign policy.

The Third Great Debate: Positivism vs. Post-Positivism

The third Great Debate of international relations scholarship was defined in terms of "positivism vs. post-positivism" or "rationalism vs. reflectionism."[4] There are really two major elements of the debate. Post-positivists (or reflectionists) have tended to side with those who argue that traditional IR theories have not taken into account a variety of non-patriarchal, excluded identities, most notably the roles of ethnicity and gender. But more importantly, at the philosophical level, post-positivism is skeptical of the positivist assumptions underlying "rationalist" (realist, liberal, and behaviorist) approaches to the study of politics: that rational, empirical observation, as utilized in chemistry and biology, can be applied to the study of politics and that grand theories (e.g., realism) can really explain the multidimensionality of world affairs. Post-positivisms have come in many forms, from deconstructivist approaches rooted in sociology (ironically called "constructivism") to normative approaches that castigate the alleged "scientific" (i.e., value-neutral) approach of realism and behaviorism. The constructivist approach has been most powerful in this third Great Debate, acknowledging that the "national interest" which preoccupies realism and liberalism is important, but asking how this interest is formed and how the national, subnational, and supranational identities that inform interests are first developed.

   The third Great Debate has had less impact on policy circles because it does not necessarily erode the utility of survey data for understanding public policy preferences over long periods of time, nor does it evaporate the need for analyzing many of the major categories that realism and liberalism continue to debate. However, the post-positivist challenge has, at least in a theoretical sense, opened the door in academe for a more thoughtful study of how the structures of international life have formed, and how they may evolve in the future. Such examinations could include religion, but almost never do. Nonetheless, it is difficult to ascertain how these deconstructionist projects will be helpful in the construction of proactive foreign policy, except to observe and admonish that actions help constitute the world. And, although constructivists have been thoughtful in arguing that ideational factors—primarily historical experience and the interaction of political entities—is what "makes" international politics, it has largely dismissed religious phenomena, largely due to its academic, secularist bias.[5]

In short, realists, liberals, behaviorists, and post-positivists have largely ignored the role of religion in global affairs. The next chapters will carefully outline why there is a secularist bias in practical foreign policy that deliberately avoids engaging and analyzing religious phenomena. However, in the aftermath of ethnoreligious warfare in the 1990s and the civilizational gauntlet thrown down by al Qaeda on 9/11, the twenty-first century is witnessing a fourth Great Debate in IR theory. On the one hand are the realists, liberals, behaviorists, and post-positivists—whether in universities or in government service—who ignore religious factors. Countering them are voices arguing that many of these paradigms can evolve to include analyses of religion, and that U.S. foreign policy must do so in order to be viable in the twenty-first century.

The Fourth Great Debate: Let Religion In?

Secularism and Religion in IR Theory

By the late 1990s, leading voices in a variety of scholarly disciplines were beginning to pursue a reassessment of the exclusion of religion in social science analyses of world affairs. Key among them was sociologist José Casanova's *Public Religion in the Modern World*, which reevaluated the myth of "separation of church and state" in Europe and its consequences for contemporary society.[6] The myth is that Europe separated church and state with the ending of the Thirty Years War (1648), and as a result, over time became more prosperous as it secularized. The problem with the myth is that it is factually wrong. Casanova demonstrates that the modern state system, birthed at the Peace of Westphalia in 1648, did not separate church and state and thus banish religion to the private sphere. Rather, it ended the notion of a mono-religious Europe, binding governments to new national churches: Catholic France, Anglican England, Lutheran Sweden, and the like. Interestingly, many Western European countries—the most secular populaces in today's world—nonetheless to this day provide tax dollars and other forms of support to these official state churches.

Casanova's reexamination of the historical record is important because it dissolved the argument of social scientists and foreign policy practitioners that highly religious societies, including those with state-sponsored churches, could not modernize and democratize—that is precisely what Europe did. Canadian philosopher Charles Taylor largely agrees. His *A Secular Age* reminds the reader that people around the world find personal and collective meaning in the spirituality, teaching, and symbols of religious faith, and thus Western skeptics cannot simply wish away the influence of religion in global affairs. Indeed, Taylor argues, it is this very sense of spiritual meaning, ethical perspective, and personal experience in a modernizing world that is key to understanding the resurgence of religion globally.[7] In short, Casanova and Taylor demonstrate that we need to rethink religion's role not only in the developing world, but in the developed as well.

More recently, IR theorist Elizabeth Shakman Hurd argues that the entire notion of "secular," both in terms of its meaning and its relationship with religion, is not a fixed historical reality, but rather socially constructed; in other words, "secular" is a Western construct, not immutable and universal law. This is a critical argument, because it means that the historical record of Western secularism is episodic, historically contingent, and evolving. Hurd argues that the scholarly community has created an artificial intellectual edifice within international affairs studies that is intentionally devoid of mainstream analyses of religious factors from theoretical perspectives. Therefore, if that paradigm is inaccurate, then societies are not predestined to secularize; there is no social science law that modernization necessarily leads to secularism, progress, and prosperity. Moreover, if there is no fixed "secularism" or a definitive political and economic tie to wealth and modernity, then new possibilities are available in the future of political development and interstate relations. Hurd points to the connections between opening IR theory to religious variables and the foreign policy challenges that religion can induce, such as the relationship of the United States to Iran as well as that of the EU with Turkey.[8] In the wake of 9/11, others have made similar arguments regarding the importance of removing secularist blinders from theory and the study of foreign policy. Timothy Byrnes and Peter J. Katzenstein argue that one of the key stumbling blocks to European integration—and thus, European security—is the salience of distinct religious and cultural identities in Eastern Europe.[9] Eric Hanson likewise problematizes rampant secularism in the IR theory. Hanson's work on globalization suggests a grand irony in contemporary global affairs: the forces that the post-World War II secular order nurtured, such as globalization, free trade, international human rights norms, information technology, and the like have aided the return of religion to the public square.[10] Of course, as Hanson notes, one of the reasons that intellectuals have been wary of religion is because it is seen as conservative, reactionary, violent, and contrary to many of the norms shared by policy and academic elite. Hatzopoulos and Petito take issue with focusing on religion solely as a driver of conflict, arguing that there are many cases where religion plays an important societal role. They say religion's return "from exile" to the global public sphere suggests that a multitude of paths are open to collectives of shared faith, including peaceful mobilization against tyranny. Interestingly, their study finds that religious justifications for mass mobilization (and sometimes violence) are generally in response to state repression and authoritarianism, as in Egypt, Syria, and elsewhere. Hatzopoulos and Petito recommend that governments and scholars take religious actors and motivations more seriously, on their own terms, in order to understand the changing global order and perhaps forge partnerships for security.[11]

It is difficult to catalog all the parameters of this fourth Great Debate as it relates to U.S. foreign policy. However, what it all boils down to is whether to continue in the tradition of the last century of U.S. thinking on international affairs and thus largely *avoid* religion, or whether to *include* religious factors in the U.S. broader foreign policy analysis. On the former side of the debate are four of the most important strategic documents that demonstrate the strategic thinking and priorities of the Obama Administration. These four documents, including the 2010 National Security Strategy and the State Department's Quadrennial Diplomacy and Development Review (QDDR), represent the thinking of the highest placed and most influential leaders in the Administration, and they largely leave religious factors out of their analysis of the world and how the United States should engage that world. In contrast, those four are followed by three recent reports—endorsed by a former Secretary of State and other thought leaders—that argue for a "Sputnik-era" level of investment in our knowledge of religious and cultural affairs.

The Princeton Project's "Forging a World of Liberty under Law"

The Princeton Project, published in late 2006, set itself no lower goal than attempting to write a new "collective X article," referring to the most famous single statement of U.S. foreign policy in the Cold War, George Kennan's article on the Soviets that outlined a policy of "containment," signed "X" by Kennan. The project, which included a long list of experts, was co-chaired by former U.S. Secretary of State George Schultz and former U.S. National Security Advisor Tony Lake, but its driving force (co-directors) were Princeton professors G. John Ikenberry and Anne-Marie Slaughter. Dr. Ikenberry previously served at the State Department and routinely consults at government agencies; Dr. Slaughter was tapped by Secretary Clinton to run the Department's Policy Planning Office, providing the primary intellectual leadership and vision within the State

Department—and thus is a critical voice for how later documents, such as the NSS and especially State's QDDR, would unfold.

The Princeton Project's *Forging a World of Liberty Under Law* identifies "protect[ing] the American people and the American way of life" as the basic objective of U.S. grand strategy, and it "should comprise three more specific aims: a secure homeland...a healthy global economy...and a benign international environment, grounded in security cooperation among nations and the spread of liberal democracy." The document went on to call for an American strategy that is multidimensional ("different tools for different situations...like a Swiss army knife"), interest-based, integrated (soft and hard power), "grounded in hope rather than fear," "pursued inside out" (strengthening domestic capacity at home and the institutions of other governments), and "adapted to the information age." The key approach to "forging a world of liberty under law" is to invest in "popular, accountable, and rights-regarding governments" abroad, deepen American relationships with global international institutions (specifically the UN, IMF, World Bank, WTO, and NATO as well as other organizations), and "rethink the role of force." *Forging a World of Liberty under Law* has much to recommend it and many of its key themes and even their specific language recur in Secretary Clinton's QDDR—written by Slaughter's office—and the 2010 National Security Strategy. What is perhaps most noteworthy is the departure from the Bush Administration's focus on *ideas,* instead emphasizing *institutions.*

However, when it comes to the role of religion in the world, the document is almost silent. Even the words "religion" and "religious" shows up less than a half-dozen times, such as "the mixture of oil, religion, ethnicity, historic grievances, non-state actors, nuclear weapons, and great power interests is so volatile that that the Middle East rivals the Balkans at the turn of the last century in explosiveness."[12] That clause alone should make the reader wonder about how religious impulses and actors could play a positive or negative role in the advancement of "a world of liberty under law." However, the document makes two key assumptions. First, when religion is in the mix, it is almost always a negative force for violence and conflict; in other words, religion is a "problem" for U.S. foreign policy.

Consequently, it is virtually unimaginable in the document that religious factors could be important to U.S. analysis or that religious actors could be allies and partners of the U.S. government. Second, the document demonstrates this secularist and negative approach to religious phenomena by making it clear—through total silence on the issue—that there are no positive links or synergies between religion and the key objectives and tools of U.S. foreign policy listed above. In sum, it is in U.S. interests to avoid religion at all costs, because of the following:

- We face many present dangers, several long-term challenges, and countless opportunities. Much is painfully familiar—ethnic conflict, religious strife, and belligerent nationalism—but much else is strangely new, including technological advances and the emergence of powerful non-state actors.[13]
- (describing the Middle East) The resulting nationalist, religious, and ethnic sentiment forces societies to close ranks and denies any space for building the pluralism, accountability, or regard for rights necessary to create stable and successful long-term societies.[14]
- Pushing into contentious religious territory to borrow various terms for subgroups or apostates is precisely to wade into the realm of religious war that we seek to avoid. Since 9/11 the Bush administration sought to convince ordinary pious Muslims around the world that America seeks no quarrel with them. The best way to start is to take Islam itself out of the equation.[15]

National Intelligence Council's Global Trends 2025

In November 2008 the National Intelligence Council (NIC) released its unclassified report, *Global Trends 2025: A World Transformed.* As the title suggests, the report forecasts the international context within which U.S. national security policy will take place over the better part of the next two decades. It is an interesting thought study, because *Global Trends* considers actual global trends and then traces the possible paths those trends may follow to different possible future scenarios. The NIC is also important because it draws on some of America's finest intellectual capital and it is widely read across universities, government agencies, and the national security-focused press, both in and outside the United States. The NIC report begins with the argument that Earth 2025 will be a "transformed" place, due to various factors including: the influence of new players on the international stage, particularly the BRIC countries of Brazil, Russia, India, and China; the long-term consequences of wealth transfer from West to East; massive population growth (an additional 1.5 billion people) and consequent pressure on natural resources, possibly leading to conflict; and the continued threat of WMDs and "political turbulence" in "parts of the greater Middle East."

One trend highlighted by the NIC is the diminution of some forms of authority and legitimacy and the rise of others. On one hand, Western centers of power and authority at both the state and interstate level will likely lose some of their standing over the next 15 years, whether it be the transfer of power from

European capitals to EU headquarters, the loss of relevancy of post-World War II institutions, or the general loss of Western cultural and institutional hegemony in arranging the international security architecture. On the other hand, in many parts of the developing world, fragile states will continue to be imperiled by their own structural inadequacies combined with increased demands for services by needy, growing populations. Those organizations that step in to fill the gap, such as faith-based health care providers, militant social actors like Hamas, or vigilantes imposing sharia as "law and order," strengthen this trend.

In short, in a world facing demographic and ecological crises and where the statist structures of the twentieth century are falling apart, the NIC asks in Chapter 6, "Will the international system be up to the challenges?" The answer is not reassuring, so the NIC further asks where people will turn for authority, life meaning, and social services. The answer may be "religion," but the NIC's framing is fairly negative: religion usually does not provide solutions or serve as an ally for Western governments and publics; religion is generally a combustible, erratic entity. In most cases, it is already causing a breakdown of the established order, even in Western Europe, as the secular welfare state is coming under financial, cultural, and religious pressure:

> Western Europe's secular, welfare state is threatened by confrontations with Muslim conservatives over education, women's rights, and the relationship between the state and religion are likely to strengthen right-of-center political organizations and splinter the left-of-center building and maintaining Europe's welfare states.[16]

Moreover, the old glue that held nation-states together, the concept of shared national citizenship, is breaking down: "intrinsic to the growing complexity of the overlapping roles of states, institutions, and non-state actors is the proliferation of political identities, which is leading to establishment of new networks and rediscovered communities."[17]

To be fair, although the first three quarters of *Global Trends* largely neglects religion entirely, and although almost the entirety of its analysis on religion is that religious actors will be the winners if the global system is in meltdown, nonetheless the NIC does nod to the important services provided by many religious actors:

> The alternative social system provided by religious organizations has been a potent factor in winning mass support for religion. This holds across faiths. The weaker the state and its mechanisms, the more critical the role of religious

institutions and the stronger the appeal of religious ideologies, usually of a fundamentalist or theocratic nature.[18]

But in general, religion is either absent from the discussion or seen as a problem or symptomatic of troubled times. Here is the express language from the NIC on religion's growing role in a transformed world.

A Growing Role for Religion. Religion-based networks may be quintessential issue networks and overall may play a more powerful role than secular transnational groupings in exerting influence and shaping outcomes in the period out to 2025. Indeed, we could be entering a new age of clerical leadership in which religious leaders become major power brokers in resolving future international disputes and conflicts...

Before 2025, some evangelists and mega-church preachers probably will seek to become the leaders of nations, especially if those countries have been economically devastated during a global downturn...

Although religious groups have been a great beneficiary of globalization, religion also has the potential to be a primary vehicle for opposition to that same modernizing process. Religious structures can channel social and political protest, especially for those who lack the means of communication and influence available to social elites. This is relevant because many of the economic trends that will dominate the next two decades have the potential to drive social fragmentation and popular resentment, including the growing gaps between rich and poor, the urban and rural gulfs in India and China, the vast disparities between nations and regions advantaged or left behind by modernization, and between states able to manage the consequences of globalization and those with governments unable to do so. Religious activists can draw on sacred texts and long historical tradition to frame popular grievances in terms of social justice rhetoric and egalitarianism. If global economic growth did suffer a severe reverse—akin to the Indonesian crisis of the late 1990s but on a worldwide scale—religiously based rural insurgencies and ethnic struggles probably would ensue in a number of countries including Brazil, India, China, and in much of Africa. If even the moderately severe projections of climate change are correct, the impacts could spur religious conflict through large sections of Africa and Asia. Among the countries at greatest risk of such conflict and scapegoating of minority communities are a number of predominantly Muslim countries with significant Christian minorities (Egypt, Indonesia, and Sudan); predominately Christian states with substantial Muslim minorities (e.g., DRC, Philippines, and Uganda) or finely balanced between Christian and Muslim (Ethiopia, Nigeria, and Tanzania).

Global Trends 2025, pp. 84–5.

The Quadrennial Diplomacy and Development Review (QDDR)

A couple of weeks before New Year's 2011, Secretary of State Hillary Clinton rolled out the first-ever QDDR, modeled on the Defense Department's long-standing mandate to publish a similar study every 4 years. The document was the result of a year and a half of evaluation, analysis, and planning; because its publication was nearly a year later than originally promised, it was keenly anticipated. The QDDR, titled "Leading through Civilian Power," aspires for a far greater role for civilian diplomatic leadership in U.S. foreign policy overseas while recognizing two constraints: fiscal austerity and the massive and dominant role that the Department of Defense has played as the primary human face of the United States abroad since at least 2001. At the press conference inaugurating the document, Secretary Clinton remarked, "The QDDR is a blueprint for how we can make the State Department and USAID more nimble, more effective, and more accountable...Leading through civilian power saves lives and money."[19]

The 200-page QDDR does assess the strategic global landscape, calling for the "elevation of diplomacy" in U.S. foreign relations, arguing that the United States must lead in "building and shaping a new global architecture of cooperation" in a world characterized by "crisis, conflict, and instability." In order to do this, the U.S. must build "a long-term foundation for peace under law through security and justice sector reform." In short, the United States must invest in the institutions of other countries, the institutions of global cooperation, and in its own diplomatic institutions; most notably in hiring more Foreign Service officers and equipping them with twenty-first century technologies.

What of religion? Unlike those who would entirely disregard non-governmental actors in international life, the QDDR acknowledges that "Non-state actors, ranging from non-governmental organizations to business, religious groups to community organizations, are playing an ever greater role, both locally and globally."[20] Thus, although religion can be "the problem," the QDDR also lists religious actors—along with a variety of other civil society actors—as possible partners: Leadership today requires us to work and partner with others in pursuit of shared objectives, starting with our traditional allies with whom we hold a longstanding community of interests and values, and including emerging centers of regional or global influence, and non-state actors from NGOs and corporate partners to religious groups and individuals.

The QDDR observes that much of the world's conflict and instability "involves multiple factions within states and is driven by a mix of religious, ethnic, ideological, political, economic, and geographic factors."[21] "In many fragile states governments are weak, institutions are struggling to serve local populations,

populations are ethnically and religiously divided, women and girls are denied fundamental rights and freedoms, and security is an ongoing challenge."[22]

So religion tends to characterize environments of division and inequality, but the reality of the global situation is that religious actors, as nodes within wider civil society, are now at least acknowledged to exist. However, although there seems to be some suggestion of "partnering," there is no commitment nor any real plan explicated in the QDDR about doing so, nor is there any commitment to develop the internal capacity at USAID and the State Department in order to understand religious dynamics or engaging religious actors. Indeed, it is hard to imagine that the Department is serious about partnering when there is virtually no mention of any of the major world faith traditions.[23] Amazingly, the document says nothing about a critical State Department function—leading U.S. international religious freedom policy—but perhaps that is to be expected as the Obama Administration did not have a Congressionally mandated U.S. Ambassador-at-Large for International Religious Freedom until May 2011, when Suzan Johnson Cook filled the post. In short, it seems clear that some wordsmith added "religious groups" to a list of other possible nonstate groups along business and NGOs, and thus if "partnering" were to occur, it would be on the instrumental basis of "using" such groups to further U.S. interests. But partnering is unlikely without investment in knowledge resources for religious literacy or political cover for those interested in these issues.

The National Security Strategy of the United States (2010)

The National Security Strategy of the United States (NSS), published in May 2010, outlines the key strategic priorities for the Obama administration. NSS are congressionally mandated documents establishing the strategic landscape, and they result (by law) in the Secretary of Defense's National Defense Strategy and the Joint Chief's National Military Strategy. These documents then become increasingly operationalized at the command and regional level in "posture statements" and "commanders' statements of intent." All of these secondary documents are for the Department of Defense alone; this says nothing about the way the intelligence community, Treasury, DHS, the Justice Department or other agencies with a piece of the national security pie respond to and operationalizes the assumptions found in the NSS. From the outset, the Obama NSS states four U.S. "enduring interests": the security of its citizens and allies, a strong economy in an open global economic system, respect for "universal values" at home and abroad, and "an international order advanced by U.S. leadership that promotes peace, security, and opportunity through stronger cooperation to meet global challenges."

These goals are consistent with their expression in past national security documents, and one can imagine a similar formulation being made by Presidents Kennedy, Reagan, or Bush.

When it comes to the strategic context of world affairs, this NSS takes the position that religion is routinely the problem. The NSS asserts that the world is "polarized" by "race, region, and religion" and that the route to peace is by replacing them with "a galvanizing sense of shared interests."[24] This negative language should not be surprising; in September 2010 President Obama told the UN that "ancient hatreds and religious divides are now ascendant."[25]

The NSS does argue that it is in America's interest to support "universal values" worldwide. These values are poorly defined in the NSS, but generally seem to mean human and electoral rights. But the values portions of the NSS say very little about the foundational experiences and ideas in the American past that undergird and inform those values, nor does it lay out a defense for the centrality of freedoms of religion, conscience, and belief to all of the other "values" in the document. Moreover, the writers of the NSS refuse to consider how promoting human liberty and religious freedom is central to American identity and—by law—should be fully incorporated in U.S. strategic policy. Religious freedom is the ultimate challenge to all forms of authoritarianism and tyranny; as President Obama declared in his aspirational Cairo speech the year before: it is those societies that protect and nourish these liberties that are the most likely to be peaceful, stable, prosperous, and representative.

Of course, applying a religious lens to America's four "enduring interests," as explicated in the NSS, indicates that there is a strategic intersection on these issues. One example is the issue of religious freedom policy in foreign policy analysis. What does it mean that the United States and its allies are not threatened by any religious liberty-loving government or group, but Americans are threatened in various ways by those who deny religious and other liberties: China, Iran, North Korea, and others? What is the nexus of religious liberty and economics? It would seem that religious freedom supports a strong economy and an open global economy based on individual freedom, the rule of law, trust, and moral behavior. Indeed, the financial meltdown of 2008–2010 is based in the erosion of the rule of law and trust in the marketplace. And religious liberty supports an "international order" characterized by peace, security, and opportunity; it is tyrannical governments and/or authoritarian religious monopolies that threaten and feel threatened by such an international consensus.

More could have been said in the NSS, and will be said in later chapters of this book about how a sensitivity to issues of religion and culture could inform the policy-making ramifications of U.S. national security, particularly when it comes to U.S. interests and lessons learned in Iraq, Afghanistan, and elsewhere; but the NSS takes the traditional, secularist approach to foreign policy, largely neglecting religion.

Mixed Blessings: U.S. Government Engagement with Religion in Conflict-Prone Settings

In August 2007 the Center for Strategic and International Studies (CSIS) in Washington, D.C. published an important report, "Mixed Blessings: U.S. Government Engagement with Religion in Conflict-Prone Settings." The study interviewed 240 foreign policy experts from a variety of disciplines in and out of government, including diplomats, academics, development specialists, USAID staff, military officers, and members of the intelligence community. *Mixed Blessings* argues that there are three critical problems for U.S. foreign policy when it comes to engaging religion in conflict-prone settings:

- U.S. government officials are often reluctant to address the issue of religion, whether in response to a secular U.S. legal and political tradition, in the context of America's Judeo-Christian image overseas, or simply because religion is perceived as too complicated or sensitive.
- Current U.S. government frameworks for approaching religion are narrow, often approaching religions as problematic or monolithic forces, overemphasizing a terrorism-focused analysis of Islam and sometimes marginalizing religion as a peripheral humanitarian or cultural issue.
- Institutional capacity to understand and approach religion is limited due to legal limitations, lack of religious expertise or training, minimal influence for religion-related initiatives, and a government primarily structured to engage with other official state actors.

Mixed Blessings succinctly demonstrates the current lack of institutional religious awareness in the United States—despite the potent effect of religious actors, identities, and transnational movements in international affairs. *Mixed Blessings* does report on a significant number of attempts by individuals and suborganizations within the U.S. government that have tried to deal with religious dynamics. Examples include the Naval Postgraduate School adding an hour on "the culture of Afghanistan" and a 90-minute introduction to the "theology of Islam" as well as the U.S. Army's revision of its chaplain training;[26] USAID's field staff collaborating with faith-based organizations, despite some skepticism at headquarters in Washington; an obscure office within the Department of State narrowly but expertly focused on Congressionally mandated religious freedom reporting. For over a decade the CIA has reached out to scholars of religion and Islam. These efforts represent just a handful of many, but they tend to be ad hoc, short term, and motivated by working-level personal initiative rather than institutionalized, resourced (human and financial), strategic, interagency, and supported by senior leaders.

Mixed Blessings also provides an in-depth case study of Nigeria—a highly religious public with deep cleavages based on religion, ethnicity, and resource competition. A stunning detail from the report comes from a Pew survey in Nigeria: 91 percent of Muslims and 76 percent of Christians say that their religious identity is more important to them than their ethnic affiliation or their identity as Nigerians or Africans. [27] The portrait that emerges from U.S. government activities is an interagency team at Embassy Abuja working very hard, and quite cleverly, to engage multiple religious and cultural dimensions of Nigerian society with some success, particularly through building personal relationships with religious leaders and modest amounts of discretionary support for conflict resolution and peacemaking efforts. However, it is clear that much of the engagement strategy was developed in an ad hoc basis on the ground in the country, not as a result of the natural course of country planning in Washington, D.C. or due to strategic coordination between the National Security Council, Foggy Bottom, and Embassy Abuja.

The CSIS report suggests that religion's influence on international affairs is poorly understood among most foreign policy experts in and out of government. Where religion is considered, it is sometimes considered to be epiphenomenal or a problem to be solved, rather than as an energetic constellation of transnational forces in the twenty-first century. Moreover, important small-scale government initiatives exist, but they tend to be short-term and ad hoc rather than integrated and interagency.

Changing Course: A New Direction for U.S. Relations with the Muslim World

Just before the 2008 presidential election, a group of 34 distinguished Americans published a call to action on U.S. relations with Muslims worldwide entitled, "Changing Course: A New Direction for U.S. Relations with the Muslim World." *Changing Course*, signed by a former U.S. Congressman, a former Secretary of State, a former Deputy Secretary of State, and other luminaries from business, universities, think tanks, and representing different faith traditions, argues that "creating partnerships for peace" between the United States and the Muslim world is both a challenge and an opportunity, and that "maintaining the status quo raises the specter of prolonged confrontation, catastrophic attacks, and a cycle of retaliation."[28]

Changing Course is an invaluable first step in not only recognizing the tensions and differing perceptions between most Americans and many in the Muslim world, but also in suggesting that the United States needs both a "whole of government" and even a whole of society approach to get at this set of concerns:

> The U.S. government, in concert with business, faith, education, and civic leaders, needs to undertake major initiatives to address the causes of tension. Working with Muslim counterparts, we can achieve substantial joint gains in peace and security, political and economic development, and respect and understanding.[29]

Changing Course provides four broad goals with recommended actions for each: (1) elevate diplomacy as the primary tool for resolving conflicts; (2) support efforts to improve governance and promote civic participation; (3) help catalyze job-creating growth in Muslim countries; and (4) improve mutual respect and understanding. *Changing Course* recognizes that the United States needs to better understand the cultural milieu of its friends and foes in the Muslim world, that the United States needs to engage religious experts and faith communities, and that it needs to drastically improve our higher education, interfaith, and outreach programs. In fact, *Changing Course* calls for "an education program comparable in scale to the post-Sputnik U.S. commitment to math and science education...The current challenge calls for an equivalent commitment to education on Islam and Muslims, sustained over a decade or more..."[30]

In conclusion, both *Mixed Blessings* and *Changing Course* make a similar, compelling argument: religion matters in key areas of the globe. *Mixed Blessings* argues that if the United States wants to help resolve conflicts in most parts of the world, it would be wise to take religion seriously. *Changing Course* makes similar claims for the Muslim world: key issues, such as American counter-terrorism strategies, are interpreted through a religious lens across much of the Muslim world, and therefore the United States would be wise to better understand the religious context of its policies (along with the cultural, political, and economic context) if it wants its strategies to succeed. If there is a Muslim world with some shared sensibilities, religion must matter. If religion is important to postconflict societies, it is likely important to preconflict societies, and therefore crucial for U.S. policy considerations.

Engaging Religious Communities Abroad: A New
Imperative for U.S. Foreign Policy

In February 2010 the Chicago Council on Global Affair's released a report, *Engaging Religious Communities Abroad: A New Imperative for U.S. Foreign Policy*. The report was the result of 18 months of deliberations by a task force of significant leaders and public servants representing the intersection of U.S. foreign policy, academe, and NGOs; and it included individuals with past experience at the Department of State, the NSC, the World Bank, and the U.S. Congress. The Task Force found that the United States is part of a highly religious world, where religious influences are intertwined with culture, economics, language, society, art, and politics, but that the United States has a mixed record—at best—in understanding and engaging religious actors, themes, movements, and ideas. *Engaging Religious Communities Abroad* lists six patterns that reflects religion's influence "in a volatile world" that mirror the patterns described in Chapter 1 of this book, including: that private and public religious voices are growing in influence in many parts of the world, that globalization benefits and transforms some elements of religion while at the same time some religious groups lead opposition to globalization's effects, that religion is used as a catalyst for violence by extremists, and the expansion of the issue of international religious freedom as a fundamental human right and source of social and political stability.

Before making its recommendations, the Chicago Council Task Force did note three major challenges to "engaging religious communities abroad." Those challenges are:

- The United States has an interest in religious communities realizing their legitimate aspirations, but must also seek to maintain its strategically important system of bilateral alliances and partnerships.
- The United States has an interest in promoting human rights, but must do it in a way that is not perceived as a Western assault on local faith and custom.
- While debates inside religious communities have a bearing on the wider world, including the United States, outsiders often lack the standing to influence them.

Clearly the authors of this report recognized the thorny, real-world dilemmas faced by American relationships with places like oil-rich Saudi Arabia and the authoritarian but antiradical Hosni Mubarak Egyptian regime, as well as how U.S. human rights and especially international religious freedom advocacy are perceived. Moreover, the United States has struggled to develop a coherent policy regarding public diplomacy and the "wars of ideas" within Islam, such as whether or not to praise and/or financially support so-called "moderates" against "extremists."

If the United States had a "mixed record" in the past, according to the report there is nonetheless some progress in some areas of government today on these issues, but the report finds them to be short term, poorly resourced, and generally ad hoc. Thus, the Chicago Council Task Force put forward two general categories of recommendations. The first is that the United States must build its internal capacity to understand the religious world it encounters in its foreign policy, and that it can do so in ways such as reforming elements of the training of Foreign Service officers as well as thoughtfully engaging the expertise of those who have deployed to highly religious environments. Second, the United States must engage religious communities effectively. More specifically, the report recommends that the United States engage not simply government-to-government, but across a wider range of societal actors. Moreover, the United States should reaffirm its commitment to religious freedom, work with international and multilateral organizations to expand and deepen their engagement with religious actors.

Conclusion

This chapter argued that the twentieth century "great debates" of international relations theory, particularly as they apply to foreign policy, largely neglected religious factors. In the academy realists, liberals, behaviorists, and post-positivists largely excluded religious variables from their models of international life, primarily due to a profound secularist bias in their approaches. When it comes to the application of theory to practice, in other words how academic thinking informs policymaking, so too religious actors and themes were largely relegated to the sidelines for most of the past century.

In those rare cases when IR theorists and foreign policy professionals did consider religion, it was typically addressed as "the problem": a driver of conflict, a tool for manipulation and coercion, or an ideational relic likely to suppress the rights and voice of women, reformers, and minorities. Indeed, the many positive influences of religion in social life—from inspiring the fight against slavery to providing an impetus for charity—were often overlooked. Finally, as discussed in later chapter of this book, in those rare cases when policy elites realized the utility of religion, such as in fighting "godless Communism" during the Cold War, religion was approached instrumentally: as a tool to be manipulated by security experts on behalf of vital U.S. interests (e.g., access to oil, competing with the Soviets).

What has changed is that particularly in the past few years a fourth Great Debate has broken out among scholars. This debate is largely one-sided: religious variables continue to be ignored by the majority of scholars, but there is a vocal minority demanding their inclusion. When one reads documents like President Obama's 2010 National Security Strategy or the Princeton Project report, it is clear that religious factors are still marginalized by many foreign and national security policy elites. However, the prominence of alternative foreign policy reports like *Changing Course* and *Engaging Religious Communities Abroad*—signed by former senior diplomats, including a past Secretary of State—suggests that new possibilities are gathering steam. The questions ahead are, first, how best to understand the secularist bias inherent in most day-to-day foreign policy thinking; second, how to reframe our paradigmatic approaches to include the multidimensionality of the religious world in which we live. Religion is not everything, but it should be something in U.S. foreign policy analysis: Americans' first task is to understand and correct that imbalance and then consider strategic, whole-of-government initiatives to implement those changes.

CHAPTER 3

The Failings of Secularist Foreign Policy Approaches

In 1964 Iran exiled a 62-year-old cleric from the country. He had spent most of his life in preparation to be a religious scholar like his father. The exile traveled first to Iraq and then moved on to Paris, long the favored destination for political cranks from around the world. He spent most of the next decade in France haranguing the "Persian" regime of Muhammad Reza Shah as anti-Islamic and in league with the godless West. Of course, he was never expected to return.[1]

However, this activist—Ruhollah Musavi Khomeini—was not content to merely retire in Paris. Throughout the 1970s he remained in close contact with activists and religious leaders on the ground and he provided a religious, nationalist, and philosophical rationale for opposing the increasingly authoritarian regime of the Shah. Many of his fierce sermons were recorded and clandestinely distributed in Iran via audiotapes, and then played at homes and mosques throughout the country. Khomeini's diatribes added fuel to Iran's fire; by the mid-1970s Iran was headed toward political upheaval as Communists, socialists, liberals, anarchists, Islamists, students, and labor unions began to make common cause in opposing the government.

How did the U.S. government assess the situation in Iran at the time? A CIA report in August 1978 assessed the Shah's regime as stable, stating: "Iran is not in a revolutionary or even pre-revolutionary situation."[2] The same year, a U.S. State Department memorandum described the relationship between Tehran and Washington as positive.[3] However, by the end of January 1979, the Shah had fled, the country was in chaos, and Ayatollah Khomeini was en route back to Iran.

Iran had been strategic U.S. ally in the greater Middle East, a counterpoise to Russian influence in the region, and an important supplier of petroleum to the West. With so much riding on Iran, how did the U.S. government fail to sense the seismic shift that was occurring in the society? How did the intelligence community not grasp the potency of religion as a tool for mass mobilization or the potential of an aged cleric to seize control of the country? How did the United States fail to forecast that the Iranian Revolution would be *the* revolution of the late twentieth century, inspiring religious movements and insurgencies across the greater Muslim world, and somehow the theocracy would endure for decades?

Part of the answer is a secularist bias in the way the U.S. government analyzed the data. It was simply not part of the Cold War-era strategic, balance-of-power analysis to take religion seriously as a key unifying factor. Strongmen in the region—Iraq's Saddam Hussein, Syria's Bashar Al-Assad, and Egypt's Nasser, Sadat, and Mubarak—were secular nationalists, not clerics. Moreover, in the Cold War context, it seemed most likely that either liberal reformers or a left-of-center coalition would collaborate in opposition to the Shah. The conventional wisdom was that modernizing, progressive Tehran was the nerve center of the country. Therefore, antimodern religious themes could not possibly provide the identity and cohesions for leading a successful opposition and ultimately transforming the regime.

In Iran, that is exactly what happened. With regard to U.S. foreign policy's default secularist assumptions, little changed for the next 30 years despite the increasing salience of religion in opposing Communism, igniting worldwide religious revivals (such as evangelical Christians in the global South), fueling ethnoreligious violence in the Balkans and Africa, and providing a religio-ideological justification for Islamist terrorism. It is only in the past few years that fledgling, ad hoc, and usually poorly-resourced efforts have been made in some corners of U.S. government agencies to develop tools and resources for understanding and engaging a highly religious world. The reasons for this reluctance to engage are at once complex and simple. In general, a reinterpretation of religion in American public life has made religion "non grata," largely due to antipathy or misunderstanding by America's academic and bureaucratic elite, thus increasingly banning religion from the public square. This radical revision of the Establishment Cause of the Constitution ("Congress shall make no law respecting an establishment of religion"), in tandem with secularist biases in the academic training of diplomats and foreign policy experts, has resulted in a foreign policy that is confused, myopic, and threatened when religious actors, arguments, and organizations enter the picture. Although the United States is characterized by a diverse, religiously vibrant population it nonetheless has largely failed in apprehending the religious undertones in its foreign policy, just as America has not organized well to engage the religiosity of others. A better understanding of our American history will provide a context for rethinking existing approaches. Following that historical review of the uniquely American approach to separating church and state, this chapter goes on to identify elements of the secularist bias that has become entrenched in most recent U.S. foreign policy: modernization theory [wrongly] predicted the end of cultural factors, including religion; separation of church and state remains a contested construct; and, as discussed in the following chapter, foreign policy "schools" fail to provide intellectual resources for engaging religious dynamics.

Religion and Government in the United States: The Myth of Strict Separation

The American notion of "separation of church" and state derives directly from experiences of European persecution in the Westphalian system. Prior to the Peace of Westphalia that ended Thirty Years War (1618–48), religious dissenters were persecuted as threats to the church; after Westphalia and the nationalization of official state churches, religious dissenters were not only heretics but also political threats, often branded as traitors to the homeland. It is noteworthy that what today we call the "Westphalian system" of sovereign states launched at more or less the same time as the American colonies: Virginia (1607), Massachusetts (1620), New Hampshire (1623), New Amsterdam (New York, 1624),[4] Maryland (1633), Rhode Island (1636), Connecticut (1638), Delaware (1638), North Carolina (1653), South Carolina (1663), and Pennsylvania (1682).[5]

More specifically, as most of the American colonists were either Dutch or English, they had witnessed this type of internecine struggle firsthand. The United Provinces (today's Netherlands) fought their own Eighty Years War, concluded as part of the wider Peace of Westphalia, to establish their independence from the Catholic Spanish-Hapsburg Empire.[6] In addition to the nationalist elements of the struggle were cultural and religious efforts for independence of conscience and worship, particularly as the Protestant Reformation had taken hold in many Dutch provinces. The Dutch experienced the penalties imposed by the Spanish crown on those who refused the Catholic faith, and their profession of religious tolerance not only became characteristic of the postindependence United Provinces but also of their colonies abroad, most notably Dutch settlement in New Amsterdam (New York). Similarly, the preceding century had seen Henry VIII's historic break with Rome, his son Edward VI's embrace of Protestantism, and then Mary "Queen of Scots'" ("Bloody Mary") accession to the throne, including a political marriage with Spain and the declaration that England was returning to Catholicism. Queen Mary's short reign laid the groundwork for civil war by installing the Heresy Acts and burning 300 religious dissenters at the stake. England's religious tug-of-war, which included nearly a century's worth of imprisonment, torture, exile, execution, and loss of property from Henry VIII through Elizabeth's reign, was the setting for some people of faith (e.g., Separatists) to leave Britain for the Netherlands and/or the New World.

Much of the population in the American colonies consisted of religious people, and the colonial governments made halting steps toward increased religious freedom. Many of the colonists despised the worldliness of the English national church, be it under the thumb of the Roman pontiff or London. Hence, as religious dissenters and reformers, they sought the opportunity to worship in the New World without the pomp and trappings of politicized religion. However, prior to 1750, these efforts were prone to fits and starts when it came to religious freedom and tolerance, such as Roger Williams' exile from Puritan (Congregationalist) Massachusetts.[7]

Although many individual colonies instituted a "state church" throughout the eighteenth century (Congregationalists in most New England colonies, Anglican in the South), still a high level of religious tolerance and opportunity for religious diversity was available, particularly in Rhode Island, Maryland, urban centers like New York and Philadelphia, and on the western frontier. This was in tune with the highly religious nature of many of the colony's communities. Hence, it was not surprising the colonials gave religious expression to their Declaration of Independence ("all men are created equal and endowed by their Creator with certain inalienable rights...") and expressly mandated in the Constitution that no religious test would be made for high office. The primary text of the Constitution had at least one other nod to religious sentiment in the presidential oath of office: the newly elected president could either "swear or affirm" to faithfully execute the office. This exception was made for those religious groups who felt compelled to eschew "swearing" and instead "affirm," per a New Testament injunction against swearing.[8]

Of course, it is in the Bill of Rights that two additional statements are made about religion, today known as the "free exercise" and "establishment" clauses. The First Amendment protects a variety of individual liberties (speech, press, assembly), declaring on religion, "Congress shall make no law respecting an establishment of religion, or prohibiting the free exercise thereof." In short, with almost no debate at the time or for much of the subsequent 150 years, the amended Constitution guaranteed the individual right to the free exercise of religion across the country, and ensured that the federal government would in no way establish a national church. Indeed, by 1789 the terms of "official" state churches, such as the Anglican Church in Virginia, were far narrower than the national churches of Europe. At the time of the Constitution's ratification, only six former colonies still had official churches, and as many scholars have pointed out, these were officially chartered state churches, but not official state denominations.[9] In other words, the state chartered an official church and provided tax revenues for its support, but in practice in most places there was a robust denominationalism (e.g., Baptist, Presbyterians) that took place outside of state structures. By the early 1800s "established" state churches were largely a relic of the past, the final ones losing their privileged status in 1818 (Connecticut) and 1833 (Massachusetts).[10] A practical "separation of church and state" within a highly religious society had developed.

The constitutional restrictions on the intervention of government in religious life were not secularism, agnosticism, or atheism in any sense of the words. The actual phrase "separation of church and state" derives from a letter by Thomas Jefferson to the Danbury Baptist Association in Connecticut.

To messers. Nehemiah Dodge, Ephraim Robbins, & Stephen S. Nelson, a committee of the Danbury Baptist association in the state of Connecticut.

Gentlemen,

The affectionate sentiments of esteem and approbation which you are so good as to express towards me, on behalf of the Danbury Baptist association, give me the highest satisfaction. my duties dictate a faithful and zealous pursuit of the interests of my constituents, & in proportion as they are persuaded of my fidelity to those duties, the discharge of them becomes more and more pleasing.

Believing with you that religion is a matter which lies solely between Man & his God, that he owes account to none other for his faith or his worship, that the legitimate powers of government reach actions only, & not opinions, I contemplate with sovereign reverence that act of the whole American people which declared that their legislature should "make no law respecting an establishment of religion, or prohibiting the free exercise thereof," thus building a wall of separation between Church & State. Adhering to this expression of the supreme will of the nation in behalf of the rights of conscience, I shall see with sincere satisfaction the progress of those sentiments which tend to restore to man all his natural rights, convinced he has no natural right in opposition to his social duties.

I reciprocate your kind prayers for the protection & blessing of the common father and creator of man, and tender you for yourselves & your religious association, assurances of my high respect & esteem.

Th Jefferson Jan 1, 1802.

The key point of this "separation," according to Jefferson, was to ensure that the individual would not have to fear state intervention in the expression of his "natural right": to worship and conscience. Nothing was said here, or in the other writings of Jefferson, Madison, or the other principal Founding Fathers to suggest the abolition of government and society from all influence of individual and collective religion; only that the state would never impose a national religion upon the citizenry. And until the mid-twentieth century, this was clearly the view not only of the populace and state governments, but also of the Legislature, the Executive, and the Judiciary.

The intent of the Founders was clear: that in America religious factionalism would not be the source of oppression, political competition, and violence that was found in Europe. Over time, the American citizenry maintained a wide spectrum of religiosity, from the minority of practicing agnostics and atheists, to the much wider range of Christian denominations accepted by the majority of the citizenry. The flood of Germans and Irish in the 1840s, and Italians and other Europeans a generation later, added to the country's religious diversity. Often the groups of these groups, such as Catholics in what had been predominately Protestant areas, often caused political controversy over issues such as public funding for textbooks and religious schools. Over time Muslims and Jews became a part of the American scene, though Christian denominations dominated for the next 200 years. A generation after the writing of the Constitution, Alexis de Tocqueville visited the United States, noting the vibrancy of its civil society and churches. He observed in 1834, "The religious atmosphere of the country was the first thing that struck me on arrival in the United States."[11] Tocqueville wisely noted the difference between the European and American experiences: in Europe, the "spirit of freedom" had been in combat with "the spirit of religion," which had been allied with the status quo. The opposite was true in the United States where the two were in harmony.

> Religion, being free and powerful within its own sphere and content with the position reserved for it, realizes that its sway is all the better established because it relies only on its own powers and rules men's hearts without external support...Freedom sees religion as the companion of its struggles and triumphs, the cradle of its infancy, and the divine source of its rights. Religion is considered as the guardian of mores, and mores are regarded as the guarantee of the laws and pledge for the maintenance of freedom itself.[12]

During Tocqueville's lifetime, French "separationism" took a radical turn, one still in effect today: *laicite*, the "militant secularism" resulting from the

French Revolution driving the Church out of the public sphere. Although *laic-ite* sounds superficially like the United States' "separation of church and state," it is fundamentally different: in the United States, "separation" restricts the government from interfering in religion, in France; *laicite* shields the government and society from the influence of religion. The French revolutionaries distrusted religion, specifically the Catholic Church, as a pillar of the *ancien regime,* resulting in numerous efforts to subjugate the Church, including government acquisition of religious properties, requiring priests to take an oath of loyalty to the Republic, and persecuting those who refused to do so. The second half of the nineteenth century saw the Church's fortunes rise and fall based on France's turbulent political climate (Church and state were officially separated in the French constitution in 1905), but *laicite* was essentially codified politically—and ultimately culturally—in French national life. The French reality is simple: religion is an absolutely private matter. It has no place in the public sphere.

The official French position today is that this separation of religion and state is the foundation of freedom for all citizens. The policy has come under fire recently as *laicite's* suspicion of religion has resulted in a ban on religious clothing and jewelry in public schools and other policies that are seen by many to prevent freedom of religious expression. Indeed in December 2008 the European Court of Human Rights upheld a ruling that a French school was able to expel two female Muslim students for wearing the hijab.[13] Supporters of the policy say that keeping religious paraphernalia out of public schools protects the rights of all students by keeping religious influence separate from education.

Much of what has been said about French *laicite* applies to Turkey's Kemalist approach to Islam. In the Turkish case, since the 1920s and the reforms of Kemal Attaturk, the government has closely controlled "official" mosques and their message through a government religion ministry (the Diyanet), and enforced a wide variety of proscriptions, most notably on dress, in public places. In short, French separationism, as well as that of its Turkish cousin, is far different from that of the United States. The American concept of "separation of church and state" is neither a fusion of religion and government (like pre-Revolutionary France) nor the exile of religion from the public square (like post-Revolutionary France). Instead, it is what Alfred Stepan has called "twin tolerations: the minimal boundaries of freedom of action...for political institutions vis-à-vis religious authorities, and for religious individuals and groups vis-à-vis political institutions."[14] Stepan's definition recognizes large roles for both religion and government institutions in American public life. The American system is one where the First Amendment to the U.S. Constitution expressly forbids government intervention in religion, but anticipates a robust, religious public. In the United States both private and public expressions of religion flourish, from acts of veneration in houses of worship to religiously inspired actors engaging in debate on major issues in politics and society. Moreover, as explicated in the First Amendment, religious liberty is part of a wider bundle of liberties that involves freedom of speech, press, and assembly. Ironically, the American "separation" provides a greater opportunity for faiths to practice than in most other systems, and it provides a formal check on the invasive power of the central government to keep it from attempting to utilize religion instrumentally for its own purpose.

In sum, from the founding of the American republic through much of its first two centuries, there was a social and legal expectation that the federal government would stay out of the religious affairs of the nation, as well as an underlying assumption that the religious character of the citizenry would influence most aspects of life—even how oaths were sworn for high office. It has only been in recent generations, largely since the 1950s, that litigation and judicial decisions have deliberately and systematically sought to exclude religious expression in the public square. Indeed, over the past half-century it has become clear that the rights of individuals and communities to express their faith and many historical and cultural representations of religion in American society have come under assault by the federal government. This has generally been through court cases or threats of lawsuit resulting in the reinterpretation of the Establishment Clause to mean that any religious content—from public prayers to Nativity scenes to Christmas carols to public meetings including religious figures—somehow violate the Constitution. This reinterpretation, often a misunderstanding by local school boards and risk-adverse junior bureaucrats, has coincided with activist courts and a secularist approach in higher education have resulted in an entire generation of college graduates and diplomats who have been instructed that religion has little place in the American public square, and that it is combustible material in international relations. In sum, it is the path toward *laicite*.

The point is simple: it is both historically inaccurate and unwise to reframe American "separation of church and state" into the antireligion, highly privatized approach now apparent in France and other countries today. It is historically inaccurate because it was never the intent of the Founding Fathers to root out religion from American public life—it was clearly a part of the lives of Washington, Adams, and many of the Founders as well as the citizenry at large for generations. With regard to U.S. foreign policy today, it is unwise for diplomats, aid experts, and military officers to be shackled by a secularist bias when pursuing the U.S. national security and foreign policy objectives, because a deliberate blindering of our eyes will only result in poor policies when we engage a highly religious world. Some of those specific causes and consequences of a secularist bias are discussed below.

Understanding the Secularist Bias in U.S. Foreign Policy

A secularist bias has become entrenched in most recent U.S. foreign policy. Princeton University professor Robert Keohane writes,

> The attacks of September 11 reveal that all mainstream theories of world politics are relentlessly secular with respect to motivation. They ignore the impact of religion, despite the fact that world-shaking political movements have so often been fuelled by religious fervor.[15]

The major philosophical assumptions undergirding the training and worldview of the current generation of foreign policy experts fail to appreciate the religious dynamics of foreign policy or disregard the religious dimension because of lack of tools, disinterest, fear, or antipathy. A major objective of this book is to identify how to begin rethinking those assumptions so that U.S. foreign policy can be just as thoughtful and nuanced with regard to religious factors as it is in many other areas. The rest of this chapter seeks to demonstrate how and why a secularist bias has become entrenched in the practice of U.S. foreign policy, due largely to the assumptions of modernization and secularization theory in the social sciences, the impact of domestic political contestation over "separation of church and state," neglect of these issues in the training of diplomats and government officials, and the failure of dominant foreign policy "schools" to provide intellectual resources for engaging religious dynamics.

Reframing Secular as Private

The classical meaning of "secular" was the social space shared by the sacred and the profane: the present, temporal world with all of its good and evil. Unfortunately, today it is used to bound religion: everything outside the narrow, formal sphere of organized religion is now "secular." There is a normative connotation in the contemporary evolution of meaning—that religious influences are not welcome outside a narrow sector; religion is entirely a private matter. The secularist bias begins by differentiating "private" morality and religious sentiments from "public" affairs; even for the religious person it compartmentalizes their "secular" work week (Monday–Friday) from what they do and experience after-hours or on the weekend. The reality is that this privatization consciously restricts religion from the wider public sphere due to concerns that religion is irrational, violent, or difficult to understand. Former Secretary of State Madeline Albright has made this point numerous times in interviews: "Diplomats trained in my era were taught not to invite trouble. And no subject seemed more inherently treacherous than religion."[16] The effect of a secularist approach on U.S. foreign policy is deliberately excluding religious factors from analysis, thereby failing to account for the diversity of religious actors and trends in international affairs. In other words, if it is beyond the pale to consider the faith-inspired motivations of India's BJP, Hezbollah, or Sri Lanka's *sangha*, then it is unlikely that America will ever be able counter their religio-ideological narratives or comprehend the root causes of their violence and appeal. At the same time, the secularist bias makes mutually productive alliances with religious actors impossible, because religiously inspired motivations and sources of authority are beyond the pale. This is the case when the United States spurns the counsel of religious "moderates" because they are religious, ignores opportunities to build relationships with prominent religious voices, or sets onerous obstacles in front of faith-based development organizations that are qualitatively different from the requirements expected of "secular" NGOs. In short, U.S. foreign policy generally does not take religion and religious actors seriously on their own terms because they are outside of the secularist paradigm.

Modernization Theory Predicted the End of Religion and Culture

Modernization theory refers to a school of thinking in studies of economic and political development that was particularly influential in the decades following the dismantling of European empires following World War II. A fundamental tenet of modernization theory expects developing societies and citizens to become secular, bureaucratic, and materialist ("rational") in outlook as they take on aspects of the industrial West. This viewpoint is rooted in the sociological analyses of the nineteenth and early twentieth century, such as Marx, Engles, Weber, Durkheim, and others. In part, it reflects the observation that as Western European societies modernized, their societies underwent transformations associated with urbanization, increased access to education, the rationalization of government and business bureaucracies, and an increasing distance between some scholars and religious faith, be it via the biblical-textual criticism of the German school or the controversies surrounding Darwinian evolution.

In sum, from the late nineteenth century onward, observers noted that, at least in Western Europe, there seemed to be a growing secularism associated with modernity. And this became a presupposition of various theories of modernization. Perhaps the best known of such theories is Walt Rostow's five phases of development. For Rostow, and many complementary theorists, "traditional" societies were characterized by traditional social structures and forms of authority, generally deriving from superstition, religion, and patriarchy. Such premodern collectives based membership and rank on kinship and other forms of organic relationship, and the economics were rural, agrarian, and precapitalist. Premodern societies entered a period of "transition" as sectors of the society gained access to modern forms of education and experience. This vanguard could provide the leadership for a country to enter the third phase, a "take-off" phase when society was led toward a modern, market- and investment-based society, including requisite evolutions in the valuing of commodities, financial goods, human capital, religious authority, and personal relationships. Countries that successfully worked through the dilemmas of "take-off," which could include wrenching changes to the social and economic order (e.g., urbanization, internal migration, and accompanying changes to family life and social values), would enter a "drive to maturity" that would include the abolition of many sectors of the economy from the traditional practices of their forefathers, most notably the establishment of modern mechanisms of science, rational bureaucracy, government solvency, and a market-based economy fully engaged in the world economy. Such a country, if it could overcome the many internal and international hurdles faced in such a trajectory, could ultimately achieve Rostow's ultimate category: "high mass consumption." In other words, the goal of Rostow's model, and that of many of his contemporaries, was a Western-style, capitalist economy in which the mass citizenry were fully engaged as citizen-consumers. It is beyond the scope of this book to discuss fully the many strengths and weaknesses of such an approach, but it is important to note that such models of modernization generally saw religious factors as impediments to development, or at the very least historical artifacts that would fall by the wayside over time as a society was enlightened by the twin beacons of self-interest and science.

"Modernization theory" was the term given these approaches in political science; in sociology departments it was termed "secularization theory." In the 1960s the most famous of the sociological analyses was found in the work of Peter Berger, such as his co-authored book *The Social Construction of Reality* (1967). Berger, and other secularization theorists, argued that religion was better understood as a relic of the past, as a set of superstitions that provided understanding for how things seemed to be. "Reification is the apprehension of the products of human activity as if they were something else than human products—such as facts of nature, results of cosmic laws, or manifestations of divine will."[17] The ramification for both the West and developing societies was clear: at best, religion was "residue" of a premodern time, and its legends and myths were no longer useful for providing meaning in the industrial age. At its worst, religion could be a reactionary, unscientific, antimodernization voice that would hamper societies from the natural, scientific course of human development. For sociologists such as Berger, the evidence in the 1960s seemed clear: religion was falling by the wayside as populaces modernized, and over time it would gradually fade away.

A generation later, religious phenomena remain potent in the private lives of people, both in wealthy countries and the developing world. When asked in 1997 about the resiliency of religion, particularly in the aftermath of the Cold War, Peter Berger gave the following assessment:

> I think what I and most other sociologists of religion wrote in the 1960s about secularization was a mistake. Our underlying argument was that secularization and modernity go hand in hand. With more modernization comes more secularization. It wasn't a crazy theory. There was some evidence for it. But I think it's basically wrong. Most of the world today is certainly not secular. It's very religious. So is the U.S. The one exception to this is Western Europe. One of the most interesting questions in the sociology of religion today is not, "How do you explain fundamentalism in Iran?" but, "Why is Western Europe different?"[18]

Berger has since been good to his word, investigating the nature of the global resurgence of religion and processes of modernization and secularization.

Many social scientists and policy practitioners, trained in Western universities, have been shocked by the reemergence of ethnic, cultural, national, and religious identities that were obscured by the ideological cleavages of the Cold War. In practice, U.S. leaders have largely continued to follow the dictates of modernization theory, thinking that economic inputs alone, such as road and school building, will advance its foreign policy objectives in religious cultures from Kandahar to Kuala Lumpur.

However, whether or not academics and practitioners are looking for religion may determine if they are surprised by religion's continuing relevance, both from a scholarly and policy perspective. In a revealing article, Jonathan Fox looked at what causes of war scholars studied when focusing on (a) the principal antagonists in the Cold War or, alternately (b) the Third World. Fox found that in the Cold War era and through the early 1990s, scholars who focused on conflict dynamics in the Soviet bloc or in the West tended to discount religion as a factor; it generally had modest effect on many of the elements of the international Cold War conflict. In contrast, scholars who studied Third World conflicts were much more likely to include religious variables in their analysis during the same period, because religious factors were much more salient in those contexts. It was the former group (former Communist countries and the West) who dominated policy debates until at least the mid-1990s. Interestingly, Fox found that by the late 1990s, many studies of conflict in the first group had taken on religious elements, often with regard to Islamist terrorism or religiously inspired insurgency (Chechnya, the Balkans, anti-U.S. terrorism, etc.). Fox concluded that part of the "resurgence" of religious factors in policy relevance and mainstream social science was that the bifurcations of the Cold War have ended, opening up not only deadly new schisms in international life, but also providing scholars with an opportunity to "see" phenomena, in this case religious factors, that perhaps they were not previously looking for or of which they were unaware.[19]

In the end, secularization theory's definition of religion as irrational, primitive, and soon to evolve into oblivion made it unworthy of major investigation for decades by other younger ranks of scholars or foreign policy experts. However, the reverse has proven true: religious factors have demonstrated a unique multidimensionality and remain deeply entrenched in identities and societies the world over. Perhaps the *New York Times Magazine* recently assessed the situation best, suggesting that American thought leaders still see political theology, particularly in its Islamic form "as an atavism requiring psychological and sociological analysis but not serious intellectual engagement."[20]

Foreign Policy "Schools" Fail to Provide Resources for Engaging Religious Dynamics

The secularist bias of modernization theory is rooted, in part, in the assumption that what drives modern, "rational" people and their politics is material interests.

This assumption is a critical element of the primary academic approaches to U.S. foreign policy, the ongoing "great debate" between realism and liberalism (liberal internationalism). The first, realism, focuses primarily on the interactions of governments as they compete for security, power, prestige, and material interests. Realists like Henry Kissinger see international affairs as anarchic, competitive, and driven by the national interest. Such a worldview generally dismisses religion as irrelevant, be it nonstate entities or the soft, but real, power of transnational actors such as Pope Benedict XVI and domestic heavyweights like Nigeria's Anglican Archbishop Peter Akinola. Thus it is not surprising that Kissinger's 900-page *magnum opus* entitled *Diplomacy* does not even have an entry for "religion" in its index; for *Diplomacy* it seems that religion's meaningful engagement with politics ended with Cardinal Richelieu in the 1600s.

Liberal internationalists are more willing to acknowledge transnational and international actors such as the United Nations or multinational corporations as well as the variety of domestic politics, but likewise give religion short shrift. Like realists, they tend to narrowly focus on materialist definitions of interests, rather than on how religious and cultural identities inform the behavior of individuals and societies. Consequently, many liberal internationalist policy prescriptions offer economic and political development (democracy) without clear reference to how such *institutions* relate to embedded *identities* and *cultures* abroad. Liberal internationalists tend to highly value political processes (e.g., dialogue, consensus-building) and focus on political outcomes, whereas many people of faith worldwide are equally concerned with first-principles and questions of ultimacy.[21]

The failures of realism and liberalism underscore why it was difficult for Washington and its allies to fully understand the religious dynamics of many movements in the twentieth century, from countervailing political Catholicisms in Latin America (conservatives vs. Leftists) to the struggle against South African apartheid. Apartheid ("apartness") was rooted in a localized, neo-Calvinist theology that claimed that separation of ethnic groups was the divinely ordained.[22] Although apartheid buttressed economic privilege and political exclusion, it must be understood as having religious overtones and deep cultural significance, and thus it was competing theological interpretations (e.g., all people are God's children) that were necessary ingredients to a broader strategy to overcome it. Not surprisingly, in the vanguard against apartheid were religious leaders. However, applied realism and liberalism only suggest that apartheid and the antiapartheid movement were only smokescreens for economic interests, not the setting for a powerful war of ideas. In the South African case it took all the levers of domestic and international power—ideas, theology, economic sanctions, mass protest, individual leadership, changing international conditions—to alter that society's course. In sum, the training of U.S. practitioners and academics in international relations and foreign policy theories is generally limited to these two important, but not all encompassing, paradigms, neither of which adequately provides intellectual tools for understanding and engaging the religious dimensions of international affairs.

Foreign Policy Practitioners Are Not Trained to
Deal with Religious Phenomena

Distinct from individual interest in matters of faith or university education in world religions is the issue of professional know-how: a government representative may or may not be personally religious but could work to develop professional understanding of faith and culture relevant to their posting. This is just as true about elements of religion and culture as it is regarding language, geography, history, or any of the areas a diplomat must delve into to prepare for a new foreign assignment. However, the U.S. government does little to prepare its diplomats for religious phenomena abroad. The secondary education of most of our diplomatic corps is law school or graduate study in international relations, steeped in the theories of realism and liberal internationalism discussed above. Many learn about economics, politics, and governance structures but unless they independently seek out specific courses in religion, they are not educated in religious contexts, the intertwining of faith and culture, religion as a collective action frame, or transnational, religiously inspired movements. Until recently "religion and politics" courses were not a significant topic in university education, and what little there is tends to still focus on sociological analyses of the so-called "Christian Right" or "fundamentalism."

Former Secretary of State Albright captured this well: "When I was secretary of state, I had an entire bureau of economic experts I could turn to, and a cadre of experts on nonproliferation and arms control . . . With the notable exception of Ambassador [for International Religious Freedom] Robert Seiple, I did not have similar expertise available for integrating religious principles into our efforts at diplomacy. Given the nature of today's world, knowledge of this type is essential."[23] U.S. aid workers, Foreign Service officers, and military personnel do receive superb professional training on many topics at the outset and at key points in their career, but this professional education is weak in preparing our personnel for engaging religious actors and publics overseas. Religion plays little role in the tradecraft courses mandatory for State Department personnel over the course of their careers. Tellingly, the last edition of a 2-year course offering guide for the State Department's Foreign Service Institute only used the word "religion" six times, generally as one of a laundry list of factors one might learn about in an introductory country-specific course.[24] To its credit, since hiring a single full-time "Near Eastern affairs" scholar in 2008, elective material has expanded, including short (but not required) courses titled *Islam—The Rise of Religion in Eurasia*; *Islam in Iraq: Religion, Society, and Politics*; and *Islam: Formation, Institutions, Modernity, and Reform.*[25]

Similarly, there is almost no formal preparation for U.S. military officers in their professional military education (PME) on such matters. PME is heavily dosed with operational training, leadership lessons, and military strategy but it generally fails to take religious factors into account at either the operational or strategic levels. In fact, existing mandatory training may be more appropriate when the model was armored divisions rolling through the Fulda Gap rather than the day-in, day-out presence of hundreds of thousands of U.S. troops in heavily religious environments where many engage daily with highly religious people.

To be fair, preliminary steps are being taken in this regard, usually by adding ad hoc, non-required material such as the National War College's once-a-year elective "Religion and World Affairs" and the Naval Postgraduate School's 90-minute introduction to the "theology of Islam." Only time will tell if these are the first steps toward systematic engagement or passing fads.

Separation of Church and State Is a Contested Construct

Previously, this chapter summarized how, for much of its history, Americans assumed a high level of religion permeating all aspects of society without any federal government intervention to support, or throttle, a specific religious group. The postwar trend, however, has been to attempt to wall off religion in the American public sphere. The effect on U.S. foreign policy has been for U.S. government officials to set aside all religious actors, themes, and issues as beyond the pale because of ambiguously defined "separation of church and state" or "Establishment Clause issues." For some, this is laziness, for others it is trepidation; a recent report by the Chicago Council on Global Affairs argued that for U.S. government personnel, the situation is muddied by conceptual haziness at the working level exacerbated by poor guidance from senior leaders.[26] The effect in government affairs, both at home and abroad, is to make government agents reluctant to acknowledge, engage, and support religious actors.

The extraterritorial application of the Establishment Clause, although perhaps not completely settled, is quite limited for a number of reasons.[27] First and foremost, the Establishment Clause is domestic in orientation: it was intended to keep the U.S. government from imposing upon or meddling in the religious affairs of the citizenry, not to banish religion from American public life. However, its domestic orientation—protecting the rights of U.S. citizens—says little to suggest that the Founders intended it to be applied to U.S. foreign policy as well. Indeed, the U.S. government has worried very little about explicit overseas support for other First Amendment liberties, such as promoting press freedom or meeting representatives of the foreign press, but many contemporary U.S. officials have been deeply skeptical of developing relationships with religious individuals and groups. When it comes to foreign affairs the Executive Branch (including the Departments of State, Defense, the intelligence community, and the like) has tremendous latitude in what it does, to whom it talks, and how it supports U.S. interests and global security.

A recent court case, *Hein v. Freedom From Religion Foundation* (2007) is demonstrative of this point. The Freedom From Religion Foundation sued the federal government in order to stop the Bush Administration's then newly established Office of Faith Based and Community Initiatives from organizing conferences to help charitable faith-based organization compete for federal funding. The plaintiffs argued that this was favoritism, thus violating the separation of church and state. The Administration countered that it was simply trying to level the playing field. The Supreme Court's decision argued that the funds expended to run the seminars were not an example of a targeted, preferential act by Congress to narrowly support religious groups, but rather an action within the discrete purview of the Executive Branch, using general discretionary funds appropriated to it. Within its own sphere, the Court argued, the Executive has considerable latitude in what it does. Referring to a previous case (*Flast v. Cohen*, 1967) which restricted tax dollars supporting domestic religious organizations, the Court decided:

> The link between congressional action and constitutional violation that supported taxpayer standing in *Flast* is missing here. Respondents do not challenge any specific congressional action or appropriation; nor do they ask the Court to invalidate any congressional enactment or legislatively created program as unconstitutional. That is because the expenditures at issue here were not made pursuant to any Act of Congress. Rather, Congress provided general appropriations to the Executive Branch to fund its day-to-day activities. These appropriations did not expressly authorize, direct, or even mention the

expenditures of which respondents complain. Those expenditures resulted from Executive discretion, not congressional action. We have never found taxpayer standing under such circumstances...*Flast* focused on congressional action, and we must decline this invitation to extend its holding to encompass discretionary Executive Branch expenditures.[28]

What should be clear is that there is much that even an expansive view of the Establishment Clause does not curtail. Establishment Clause concerns do not limit U.S. foreign policy experts from training on global trends in religion as well as targeted, comprehensive religion, culture, and language preparation prior to an overseas deployment. It does not limit U.S. government officials from building enduring relationships with religious communities in foreign settings, it does not limit dialogue and respectful disagreement with people of faith in foreign publics, it does not keep us from promoting religious freedom and interreligious dialogue, nor should it deter us in any way from thoughtfully evaluating religious phenomena that affect U.S. foreign policy.

However, as discussed in Chapter 2, a recent study by the Center for Strategic and International Studies (CSIS) reports,

> U.S. government officials are often reluctant to address the issue of religion, whether in response to a secular U.S. legal and political tradition, in the context of America's Judeo-Christian image overseas, or simply because religion is perceived as too complicated or sensitive...[and] institutional capacity to understand and approach religion is limited due to legal limitations, lack of religious expertise or training, minimal influence for religion-related initiatives...[29]

The CSIS report suggests that religion's influence on international affairs is poorly understood among most foreign policy experts in and out of government. Where religion is considered, it is sometimes considered to be epiphenomenal or a problem to be solved, rather than as an energetic constellation of transnational forces in the twenty-first century. Moreover, important small-scale government initiatives exist, but they tend to be short-term and ad hoc rather than integrated and interagency.

What is needed is an investment in religious literacy, in religious expertise, and engagement of America's unique religious capital. However, a major reason why that is not happening is due to the self-imposed limitations in the theoretical constructs upon which most U.S. foreign policy is based, and in which the vast majority of U.S. foreign policy experts are schooled: the perspectives of realism and liberal internationalism. The next chapter examines these Western perspectives on IR theory and foreign policy, demonstrating that in general they neglect religious factors in global affairs, but both schools have the internal resources to widen their analyses to include religious actors, themes, and phenomena.

CHAPTER 4

New Opportunities for Liberalism and Realism

Shortly after taking office as U.S. Secretary of State, Hillary Clinton visited Mexico City to hold talks with senior Mexican officials. Following those talks, Secretary Clinton made an unscheduled visit to Mexico's holiest site, the Basilica of Our Lady of Guadalupe.[1] The profound religious and cultural significance of the site is difficult to overestimate: every year 18–20 million people pilgrimage to the basilica, many traveling miles on their knees in veneration. The sacred space dates to events in December 1531, when a local peasant named Juan Diego claims to have been visited by the Virgin Mary. Diego was instructed to tell the local bishop to build a church on that spot. The local bishop doubted Diego and asked for a sign. When Juan Diego returned to the site, he was again visited by Mary who told him to gather roses and return to the bishop with them. Even though it was winter, Spanish roses immediately blossomed at his feet and Diego plucked handfuls of them, carrying them in his *tilna* (cloak) back to the bishop. When Diego approached the bishop, not only did he have the roses in hand but a miraculous image of Mary had been painted by the hand of God inside of his *tilna*.

Juan Diego's *tilna* remains on display today at the church built on that holy site, the Basilica of Our Lady of Guadalupe. Not only has it survived nearly 500 years without sign of decay, but it has also survived war, earthquakes, and even a bomb blast set off just a few feet away. It is believed to have been the focal point for hundreds, or perhaps thousands, of cures and miracles. Every Mexican understands the significance of the *tilna*, as do millions of Catholics throughout the Americas.

Thus, it was entirely appropriate for Secretary Clinton to make a respectful visit to Mexico's most famous and sacred site, although she herself is not a professed Catholic.

However, to some observers, what was shocking was the moment when Secretary Clinton asked a question of profound ignorance: "Who painted it?" The bishop simply answered, "God." How is it possible that the U.S. Secretary of State could visit one of America's two closest neighbors and display an utter lack of knowledge and appreciation for that country's most important cultural and religious icon? Indeed, how is it possible that almost no senior American officials ever visit, as a signal of respect and interest, the single most important religious site in North America? Why was it not on the Secretary's itinerary in the first place, when on the same trip she visited a biogas plant, a regional university, and a roundtable with indigenous students at a museum?

The answer to these questions has to do with the secularist bias in U.S. foreign policy discussed in the previous chapter. More specifically, a secularist approach to the itinerary of senior U.S. officials would of course avoid religious sites because it would generally not think to add them to the itinerary—nor brief the Secretary of their significance—in the first place. Part of the reason for this is how the academic discipline of international relations theory informs the ideas undergirding U.S. foreign policy. This chapter looks specifically at the two principal approaches to applied international relations theory, realism and liberalism (liberal internationalism). As Chapter 2 mentioned, the "great debate" between these two paradigms continues to inform not only theory, but the actual practice of U.S. foreign policy on a daily basis. Unfortunately, both fail to extend their analyses to religious leaders and authority, faith-inspired action, and other religious factors. However, both schools of thought do have the internal resources to reform and provide better policy analysis and guidance on a world characterized, in part, by a global resurgence of religion.

Liberalism's Religion Problem

What is liberalism or liberal internationalism? According to Michael Lind,

> The ideal of liberal internationalism therefore is a world organized as a peaceful global society of sovereign, self-governing peoples, in which the great powers, rather than compete to carve out rival spheres of influence, cooperate to preserve international peace in the face of threats from aggressive states and terrorism.[2]

There are a number of key ideas in this definition. The first is that this is a non-isolationist approach to international life based explicitly on assumptions of contemporary liberalism (e.g., rule of law, human rights, the possibility of cooperation) and the presupposition of their applicability to international life. Second, those "sovereign, self-governing peoples" are representative polities.

Such democracies base their legitimacy not on cultural expression, ancient myth, religious faith, nor on brute power, but on the institutionalized expression of self-determination through the rule of law. In other words, these republics are characterized by shared institutions. Third, *à la* Kant and Woodrow Wilson, international relations can be an international society, not anarchy, in which great powers cooperate via rules and norms in pursuit of collective security. Interestingly, at least in this definition, contemporary threats come from "aggressive states and terrorism": what specifically is it that drives these contemporary threats?

At issue is whether or not such an international system of shared sovereignty and responsibilities is up to the intellectual and policy tasks of understanding and engaging the religious phenomena in international life. Unfortunately, the ideational superstructure of contemporary liberalism fails to adequately account for many of the issues that religion brings to international politics, including questions of secularism, legitimate authority, interests, first principles, and a libertarian moral perspective.

Legitimacy

A key principle for liberals is that of *legitimacy*. For liberals of the Kantian and Wilsonian schools, political legitimacy tends to rest with the *vox populi* (voice of the people), or some version of popular sovereignty and self-determination. In theory, the leaders who represent political collectives should be popularly elected, and those are the appropriate individuals with whom Washington should engage. Liberals are willing to take this a step farther and recognize that international life does increasingly include other voices, such as (secular) non-governmental organizations, but in general international affairs is the purview of elected representatives meeting bilaterally or even in multilateral venues to ensure collective security.

The principle of legitimacy can be very different in highly religious societies for two reasons. First, as a practical matter, many governments around the globe simply are not legitimate in the eyes of their populace, but they remain the primary interlocutor for Western governments. This illegitimacy may be the way that they came to and retain power lacked popular support or because those governments are absent, corrupt, violent, and/or rapacious. Nonetheless, it is the illegitimate leaders such as Zaire's Mobutu Sese Seko and Zimbabwe's Robert Mugabe who retain their nation's seat at the United Nations year after year.

Second, and more importantly, many societies have important figures with widespread, real legitimacy that derives from a source other than elections. Nigeria, Africa's most populous nation and perhaps the world's most religious country, is a case in point. Nigeria's democracy is at best fragile, its previous president was irrelevant from the day of his inauguration due to illness, and it is riven by economic, social, political, ethnic, and religious discord. Despite widespread dissatisfaction with the national government, Nigeria does have widely legitimate social actors, particularly within its religious groups. Two of the most important figures are the Sultan of Sokoto and the Anglican Primate of Nigeria. The sultanate, Nigeria's 200-year old caliphate, represents 70–80 million Nigerian Muslims as well as others in West and Central Africa. The current sultan, Muhammad Sa-ad Abubakar, spent 31 years in the Nigerian military, including as the defense attaché in Pakistan and in various peacekeeping operations, before assuming the position upon his brother's demise.[3] The Primate, Nicholas Okoh (and especially his predecessor Peter Akinola), speaks for not only Nigeria's 17 million Anglicans but a much-wider group of local Christians and Anglicans worldwide, particularly on social issues like marriage and the family.

The inability of liberal internationalism to comprehend and engage the religious sources of legitimacy is out of touch with reality and can significantly damage American interests. The 2003 invasion of Iraq exemplifies this: the Coalition was little prepared for the ethnoreligious tsunami that was unleashed by victory in the "hot phase" of the war. The United States wisely realized the importance of Iraqis taking the lead after the fall of Saddam Hussein, but unwisely relied on a secular Iraqi exile, Ahmed Chalabi, to head that effort. When one of the few religious clerics that the United States recognized, Abdul Majid al-Khoei (son of Iraq's most revered cleric of the previous generation), was assassinated shortly after his return to Iraq from exile abroad—allegedly by associates of another Shia cleric, Muqtadr al-Sadr—the United States was bereft of alternatives to quickly replace him. Coalition Provisional Authority czar Paul Bremer decided to eradicate Iraq's functioning governmental structures (e.g., the army and the Baathist party) in order to build from the ground-up a rational, Western-style, liberal government. The United States did not seem to know who Grand Ayatollah Ali Sistani was, but Paul Bremer quickly learned. Sistani was the successor to al-Khoei's father, and although distinctly apolitical, had been imprisoned by Saddam Hussein. He was, and is, a revered senior Shia cleric with impeccable religious and scholarly credentials. Sistani was not political per se, but he single-handedly forced Paul Bremer's hand on timely national elections in 2004 and later was responsible for numerous peace overtures, including diffusing without bloodshed the dire situation when Muqtadr al-Sadr's forces barricaded themselves in a Najaf mosque in the summer of 2004. Grand Ayatollah Sistani's influence is based not on an election or arms but on his academic and religious credentials as well as his leadership over various educational and charitable foundations (worth millions of dollars). Sistani, Muqtadr al-Sadr, and other clerics have widespread legitimacy and continue to play key roles in Iraq, unlike most secular alternatives like Chalabi. Unfortunately, it was not until 2007 that religious actors were systematically engaged by Coalition governments on behalf of peace and security.[4]

Finally, the issue of legitimacy and authority increasingly transcends borders. Liberals have done a better job than realists, who tend to focus solely on state actors in academic analysis, in recognizing that a globalized world includes a variety of nonstate actors. Nonetheless, the literature and practice of liberals tends to focus primarily on secular NGOs (many of whom have observer status at the United Nations and are routinely consulted). What is largely absent from such considerations is the widespread legitimacy and activity of transnational religious actors, such as the Roman Catholic Church or the loose network of al Qaeda affiliates worldwide.[5]

Interests

Like realists, liberals tend to focus much of their analyses of international life on interests. For many realists, international affairs is a competitive zero-sum game in which the pursuit of national interests is likely to result in conflict. For most liberals, interests do drive international relations, although the pursuit of the national interest may result in mutual gains through trade, diplomacy, and cooperation.

What is shared by both realists and liberals is a narrow, materialist definition of interests. Liberals assume that states, regardless of regime type, are primarily motivated by economic and security goods, and thus are rational actors with which others can reason. This means that any political actor operating from some other principle of interest is, by definition, irrational. For liberals this tends to result in a set of policy prescriptions that offer economic and political development (democracy) as the "solution" to the dilemmas and disagreements of political life world-over.

What is missing is how religious and cultural identities inform the behavior of individuals and societies: identity informs interests. For instance, religion and culture may induce or exacerbate conflict. Such is the case in Lebanon, where continuing war is in nobody's interest yet violence remains endemic. Religious inspiration also motivates the Lord's Resistance Army in Uganda, the ELN in Colombia, and influential figures in and out of the governments of the Philippines, Indonesia, Pakistan, Brazil, Iran, and elsewhere. Indeed, religious identity can transcend material interests, as demonstrated by suicide bombers in Baghdad or Catholic priests who venture alone into Colombia's jungles in the hope of securing the release of hostages. In other words, liberals have a world-view and accompanying policy recommendations that do not take into account embedded religious identities and cultures abroad. Liberals tend to assume that religious people can be "bought off" with economic development packages and that religious motivations and identity can be explained away in terms of class and race.

Outcomes vs. First Principles

Liberal internationalists tend to highly value political processes, and for good reason. The achievements of international law and organizations have been hard fought over a long period of time. Political processes, particularly those of deliberation, hearken back to Kant's *Perpetual Peace* in the notion that representative forms of government—by their very nature and processes—are less likely to go to war. This is primarily because the transparent, methodical nature of deliberative processes allows the public (including voters, journalists, etc.) to weigh in on the question of national interests and war. Enshrining these processes in international life through the United Nations and other global mechanisms is an important liberal goal.

However, the reality of contemporary diplomacy is that process has become an end to itself. NATO intervened in Kosovo in 1999 because the process for thwarting genocide was stalled; nonetheless there are many liberal voices who called the intervention "illegal." Similarly, there was a vast array of procedural issues that slowed the 2003 Coalition invasion of Iraq, a country in violation of 17 UN resolutions and hit with economic sanctions that did little to affect the regime or national elite.

For liberals, it is the political process and pragmatic outcomes that matter. For many diplomats, processes such as "raising the issue" or holding a meeting can be labeled a success in and of itself. Similarly, there are many issues that the pragmatic consensus at UNICEF, the WHO, or other liberal bodies, that what matters is implementing a process for service delivery. Issues such as infant health, maternal health, birth spacing, reproductive rights, abortion, family planning, and population control represent one particularly thorny set of interrelated moral issues for religious people; for many liberal internationalists the issues are simply development problems to be solved.

For religiously motivated individuals, processes are not what matter most. Principles do. People of faith tend to be interested in more than the least-common-denominator policies that result from processes and consensus. Rather, many people of faith worldwide are equally concerned with first-principles and questions of ultimacy. The questions of human flourishing, justice, the rightly ordered society, and maintaining right relationship with God and his laws are critical in religious society. Hence, religious actors can take a very different view on some issues from the Western, secular consensus, based on the moral and theological implications of proposed policies. Religious faith, regardless of whether an outside "expert" agrees or disagrees with it, has significant potency in many places and is a force for the legitimization of ideas. Consider, for example, the recent issue of polio vaccinations in Pakistan. *Foreign Policy* magazine reported:

> Pakistan's largest Islamist umbrella group, the Muttahida Majlis-e-Amal (MMA), issued a *fatwa* in January 2007 endorsing the provincial government's efforts to immunize children from polio in the country's Northwest Frontier Province. But even though health workers carried copies of the ruling with them as they trudged across the province, *The Guardian* reported in February 2007 that the parents of some 24,000 children had refused to allow the workers to administer polio drops. It turns out that influential anti-state clerics had been issuing their own *fatwas* denouncing the campaign as a Western plot to sterilize Muslims. Although Pakistan only saw 39 cases of polio last year [2007] and most children have now been immunized, a similar religiously motivated firestorm against polio drops in Nigeria in 2003 allowed the eradicable disease to spread to 12 new countries in just 18 months.[6]

Similar instances of a religious "urban legend" regarding polio vaccinations at that time have been reported across the border in Afghanistan and in Nigeria.

In short, religious themes provide a foundation for not only the transcendent, but for everyday morality and ethical challenges within and across societies. Liberal approaches that only appeal to a materialist, this-worldly, short-term set of interests fail to understand the wider range of appeals to legitimacy that are consonant with the human intellect and the human spirit. Liberal approaches, when devoid of an appreciation for the nuances and depth or religious and ethical sentiments, are likely to result in negative unintended consequences, particularly on social issues.

Liberty as License

A problem for Western foreign policies that define themselves largely in terms of "human freedom," "rights," and "empowerment" is the fundamental definition of liberty. This is particularly a problem for the collection of liberal approaches to international affairs as they craft policy at the national and international level. More specifically, the agenda of Western liberal internationalism appears to many religious individuals to have a swollen definition of freedom. Liberty seems to have become licentiousness in Western societies—the notion that anything goes, and that the individual has absolute freedom to think, say, do, or be anything that he or she wants. This contrasts with the traditional obligations within more collectivist, obligatory, kin-based societies common in the Near and Far East. Moreover, if the West suggests that Western-style "social" freedoms are desirable everywhere (e.g., legalized divorce, abortion, promiscuity, violence, pornography, homosexuality, drug abuse, lack of familial responsibility for the elderly), millions in other cultures demur, "no thank you."

In other words, this libertinism rejects notions of individual duty or obligation either to state institutions or to social ones (e.g., family, kin, tribe, collective), and thus not only portends the apocalypse to medieval mullahs like the Taliban, but is foreign and threatening to hundreds of millions of people for whom notions of collective identity and responsibility are important. Western policies that promote, or even simply broadcast, a hedonistic or atomistic liberalism will continue to cause resistance and resentment in other parts of the world.

More specifically, this chapter is not discussing the social commentary directed against the world's most watched television show (Baywatch) or the denunciations by foreign religious leaders about the culture wars going on in the United States. Rather, it is when increasingly libertine definitions of human freedom are promoted via international organizations or as the strings attached to foreign aid that Western foreign policies can—and have—experience(d) a backlash. And liberal international projects—ones that see the world as improving and safer only when other countries have Western-style democratic governments—are susceptible to the "civilizing" mission.

Hence, international pressure on highly religious societies for "progressive" divorce laws, for access to abortion, for expansive definitions of appropriate (or entirely privatized) sexual mores, and most recently, on behalf of gay "marriage"

smacks of cultural imperialism and is likely to play into the hands of authoritarian "protectors" of the status quo. Indeed, two related events demonstrate
the global nature of such culture wars today: in December 2009 Uganda proposed legislation to impose draconian punishments on homosexuals igniting a
firestorm in Western capitals and the United Nations in the same month that
Secretary of State Hillary Clinton defined the freedom "to love in the way that
they choose" (i.e., gay marriage) as a sacred right on par with religious liberty.[7]
It is hard to imagine that a realist like Henry Kissinger would find involvement
on such issues as important to the U.S. national interest; in contrast, it is easy to
imagine that Orthodox priests, Catholic bishops, Muslim imams, and millions
of religious people worldwide find such sentiments troubling and central to how
they view American influence in their region.

Democracy

The liberal internationalism associated with Woodrow Wilson in the early
twentieth century was not focused on domestic democratic mechanisms, but
rather on the rights of peoples to self-determination. Certainly Wilsonian liberalism privileged representative forms of government, but it was more interested in how self-determination was a reflection of legitimacy and popular
sovereignty. Thus, conceivably a monarchy and other forms of government
could be legitimate if in accord with self-determination. Today, such conservative conceptions of international life no longer vitiate the policy implications of liberal internationalism. On the one hand, there remains a strong
push toward supranational governance and international institutions among
many liberal internationalists. At the same time, a great deal of policy energy
is expended on resourcing domestic institutions within developing societies,
such as Western-style judiciaries and legislatures, regardless of the evidence
about whether or not such investment pays dividends in the long run.[8] This
brings the discussion back to the fundamental question, and a profound disagreement, about the nature of democracy itself. Is democratic government,
in its varied forms, the highest form of human political achievement? In other
words, is contemporary democracy an expression of human reason, the ability
for social progress to overcome past inequality: is it in accord with humanity's
better angels? Furthermore, can a religious society rely on the sovereignty of
the people?

   If democracy is perceived, or sold, as popular sovereignty and the ability of the masses to vote on laws (and thus morality), then democracy will
not find favor with many religious people, particularly conservative Muslims.

A critique throughout many quarters of the Muslim world is that there can be no popular sovereignty, because Allah is sovereign. Thus social structures and governments must be completely dependent on divine revelation; any form of popular sovereignty is blasphemy. Furthermore, if elections, polls, and referenda suggest that "we the people" are actually writing the law, and thus putting into effect its own standards of ethics, such is likewise unacceptable. Many Muslims, as well as people of other faiths, believe that laws proceed from the moral principles articulated in their faith traditions, not popularity contests or public opinion. The point here is not that democracy is inappropriate for highly religious, particularly Muslim-majority, societies. Instead, the point is that a secularist approach to democracy promotion that gives short shrift to the cultural relevance of authority, legitimacy, morality, and representation is likely to needlessly undermine support for human liberty and democratic governance.

There are alternative arguments for democracy that are consonant both with realism and the worldview of highly religious societies. It is expressed in Winston Churchill's aphorism, "Democracy is the worst form of government, except for all of the other forms that have been tried" and James Madison's maxim in Federalist 51 that "men are not angels." Christian realist Reinhold Niebuhr, recognizing human potential and human sin, observed, "Man's capacity for justice makes democracy possible; but man's inclination to injustice makes democracy necessary."[9] Niebuhr's fundamental principle of practical democracy is not one of political equality, suffrage, or individual liberty. Rather, it is the institutionalization of checks on power. Democracy checks the license of the governed with the rule of law and formalizes mechanisms for distribution of authority and resources. Democracy likewise checks the power of factions and communities and similarly limits the power even of government authorities. Niebuhr argued, "the democratic techniques of a free society place checks upon the power of the ruler and administrator and thus prevent it from becoming vexatious."[10] He cited Madison's caution about factions, and points to the three great divides in Western public life: ethnicity, religion, and class.[11] Niebuhr recognized that it is only in democracy that these competing claims can be adjudicated and that the interests of all be partially served. In fact, it is only in democracy that groups can safely call for change, and at times get it, without resorting to revolutionary upheaval. These "checks and balances" are power politics of the realist variety; they are pragmatic in their appreciation of the need to balance power with countervailing power and allow for peaceful conflict. However, these are also justifications for democracy that ring true to religious societies: the rule of law, checks on government power (including over religious practice), formal mechanisms for conflict resolution, and individual rights (including to worship).

Realism's Religion Problem

What is Realism?

Realism is the long-standing opponent of liberalism in IR theory and in practical foreign policy. It is a tradition with an impressive lineage: Thucydides, Machiavelli, Hobbes, and in the twentieth century Niebuhr, Kennan, Morgenthau, Kissinger, Waltz, Mearsheimer, and others. Over the past generation of scholarship, a variety of realisms have developed: neorealism, structural realism, offensive realism, defensive realism, and the like.[12] Most importantly, realism is not simply a theoretical exercise engaged in by academics in ivory towers; it is the foreign policy creed of many of America's most senior elected officials and national security experts: Secretaries of Defense Robert Gates and Donald Rumsfeld; National Security Advisors Jim Jones, Condoleeza Rice, and Brent Scowcroft; Secretaries of State James Baker and Colin Powell; and many others at the White House, National Security Council, and various federal agencies. Indeed, many presidential administrations, including those of Reagan, Bush, and Obama, have promised a return to some elements of realism in their foreign policies prior to taking office.

What is realism? It is a theoretical and foreign policy perspective that sees international relations as anarchic, competitive, and self-interested. More specifically, realists tend to understand international relations as characterized by the lack of central authority (anarchy), and thus it is up to individual states to pursue what is best for them and their citizens. This principle of "self-help" suggests that, in a world of finite resources, states are responsible to garner the elements of national power and material resources necessary for their countries to succeed, and thus states will likely come into conflict. Indeed, most realists see competition and struggle as the enduring principles for change and development in international relations, whether it be economic competition, political one-upmanship, or outright war. For many realists, influenced by views of human nature ranging from the religious to the Social Darwinian, this struggle for the fittest to survive and thrive is rooted not simply in the architecture of international relations, but in the moral and psycho-physiological makeup of humanity itself.

The notion of power underlies most realist analyses: the ability of states to acquire what they need (and desire), the capacity to influence other states to do what they want, the ability to defend one's country and one's way of life, the capability to deter threats and defeat rivals, and the persuasiveness to shape international norms in accord with one's point of view. Power is fungible: it has explicit military and financial dimensions, but in the twenty-first century these capabilities are demonstrated through a wider array of tools of national and social power beyond traditional land armies and domestic manufacturing capacity; such as cyberspace, prestige in international organizations and alliances, and intellectual capacity in the information age. With this in mind, many describe realism as a "zero-sum game": that there can be only a sole winner in any international political "transaction," be it a trade agreement or war. This may be too simplistic a portrait of realism, but it is true that the perspective believes that it is up to governments to do the best that they possibly can to pursue and promote their interests in a competitive world. In other words, for most realists, perceived weakness is provocative in international relations because it signals to competitors an opportunity to alter the status quo in their favor. Hence, states are left with a security dilemma: in conditions of anarchy and uncertainty they must pursue their national interests in a world of limited resources and hazy information while balancing material interests and legitimate defensive needs against the possibility that their actions and interests will likely result in increased chance of conflict.

As discussed in the previous chapter, secularism is a critical assumption of most international relations theories and applied foreign policies today. For realists, competition among states in a self-help, anarchic world is the critical reality, and whether or not individual humans and groups identify with a religious faith or not, realists contend that the struggle for power, prestige, and resources remains the same and thus ideational factors like religion, culture, and ideology generally have not mattered for foreign policy analysis. However, with all of realism's strengths it nonetheless has been consistently blind to the powerful role of religious factors in shaping the context of international affairs in recent decades. Realists could not imagine how Iranian zealots could overthrow the Shah much less run a country of 75 million people for three decades; realists find it difficult to explain suicide bombers and jihadists; realists cannot understand why governments in Afghanistan, Pakistan, and elsewhere deliberately provoke their Western benefactors—to the possible detriment of their material interests—by crushing religious liberty and human rights; nor can realism fully explain the religiously inspired bloodlust of the Balkan wars nor the faith-inspiration that motivates Mennonites, Quakers, and others to pursue peace initiatives in the most dangerous of locales. However, as in the democracy discussion above, there are areas where an expansion of realist analysis could provide new insights as to religious phenomena in international affairs, particularly in the areas of power, interests, and the formation of values.

Power

All realists agree on the centrality of power to theoretical and policy approaches to international affairs. Scholars study how power develops, shifts, grows, and wanes in international life and how actors vie for it, often through various forms of balancing activities. Because power is fungible, it can take different forms over time and space, although its various manifestations are neither equal nor always immediately transferable. In fact, realists have an explanation for the development of liberals' favorite institutions, international law and organizations: such are the tools by which the weak attempt to constrain (balance) the strong.

It was only a generation ago that arch-realist Josef Stalin asked, "How many divisions has the pope?" Stalin made the mistake that many realists make, equating power solely with states and material capabilities. However, it was a Catholic pope who helped lead a normative and ideational struggle against Communism in Europe, particularly by nurturing Polish Catholic identity and the political organizing that eventually became Solidarity in Poland.[13] Today it is far more common to see religious actors demonstrating various types of power, from mobilizing mass demonstrations to collecting and disbursing large sums of money to commanding violence.

Traditional realist theory focuses on the military and financial capacity of states, and thus focuses on major powers (e.g., the United States, European Union, Russia, China) and well-armed potential spoilers (e.g., North Korea, Iran). Hence, a country's foreign policy is generally informed by analyses of army size, technological capacity, the presence of WMDs, and measures of economic robustness. However, none of these measures adequately capture the potency of religious factors as transnational motivators for action or as domestic sources of influence and legitimacy.

In other words, a power politics foreign policy tends to operate government-to-government, focused on traditional sources of national security and diplomatic exchange. Such will do little to provide national leaders with an understanding of the motivations of international groups, such as al Qaeda, who are motivated by a religious ideology. Moreover, traditional diplomacy does little to understand and engage the nongovernmental shapers of public opinion in highly religious societies like senior clerics in the Middle East and Africa.

Realism needs to refocus its attention to consider the growing influence of religion in international affairs. An intellectually honest realism would be constantly seeking to identify and analyze fluctuations in power in domestic and international life. And in the contemporary era, religious actors, ideas, and institutions are increasingly powerful. True, some forms of realism do look in domestic society and transnational affairs and, instead of focusing on formal governance structures, identify the mechanisms and actors who in fact hold the power. Today, such actors in many countries have a religious rather than strictly political basis for their authority and legitimacy. This is true for many of the actors identified earlier in this chapter, including Anglican prelates, the Sultan of Sokoto, Grand Ayatollahs Ali Sistani and Khameini, and the like. However, it is not just individuals and transnational groups, such as al Qaeda, who hold and exercise religious and other forms of power. Indeed, an innovation of the past 20 years is the increase in state-level claims to legitimacy based on religious inspiration, particularly throughout that part of the world that just a few years ago embraced secular "Arab nationalism." A contemporary realist research agenda should further explore not just the individuals and groups who hold such power, but how religiously inspired forms of authority and legitimacy are similar to and different from others, be they resource-based or ideological. Such analyses would not merely be a theoretical exercise; they could provide valuable insight for U.S. foreign policy professionals.

Interests

Contemporary students of international relations need look no further than President Obama's 2010 National Security Strategy to find an explication of America's four "enduring interests": the *security* of its citizens and allies, a *strong economy* in an open global economic system, respect for *universal values* at home and abroad, and "an *international order advanced by U.S. leadership* that promotes peace, security, and opportunity through stronger cooperation to meet global challenges."[17] Realists, who define interests in terms of the needs and desires of the country (e.g., energy security, freedom from threat of attack, a robust economy, etc.), can easily demonstrate that these "enduring interests" can best be understood by realism's notions of power politics and self-help: the U.S. government must promote and defend the lives, livelihoods, and way of life of the American people, and this is best served in an international order conducive to U.S. influence and the values which benefit Americans on the global stage, such as the rule of law (e.g., over intellectual property rights) and global capitalism.

However, where realism falls short is in defining and explaining the wider set of interests that motivate individuals, collectives, and governments. Realism tends to assume a "rational actor" model of behavior, presuming that individuals as well as polities operate principally on behalf of material interests. This approach does little to understand the motivations of self-sacrificing individuals such as suicide bombers or of various types of groups who donate time and money across borders to enhance the well-being of foreign societies. More importantly, U.S. diplomats who operate solely from a realist perspective will little understand how the societies they engage define and interpret their interests and how such interests inform the foreign policy of those regimes, unless they consider religious factors, from the voices of influential clerics to societal mores—influenced by faith—that inform the national interest. In contrast to the "rational actor," Douglas Johnston calls this "the whole actor" model.[15]

An example of this blazed across world headlines in 2010 as Uganda knowingly risked international sanctions by promulgating tough laws against homosexuality; despite Western criticism, however these laws were popular with a majority of Ugandans due to the highly religious nature of their society. Similarly, it is difficult to understand the motivations of Sri Lanka's government without understanding their Buddhist notion of the *sangha*; the nuclear stand-off between Pakistan and India cannot be fully comprehended without considering Pakistani Islamic nationalism and reactionary *hindutva* in India; the policies, squabbles, and agendas of Tel Aviv, Beirut, Gaza, and the West Bank all are influenced by religious actors and religious considerations; and one cannot divine how interests are defined in Iran without plumbing the theology of its clerical elite. In sum, realists are right that interests matter, but a twenty-first century approach to foreign policy must consider the ideational and religious factors that inform the national interest in highly religious societies.

Morality, Liberty, and License

The realist tradition generally operates from the position that *realpolitik* is the ethics of international statecraft. In other words, the morality of international life is that states must do what they deem necessary in pursuit of the national interest. Thucydides captured this in the Melian Dialogue, when the Athenians told the isolationist Melians, "the strong do what they can and the weak suffer what they must."[16] Machiavelli also captured this perspective in *The Prince*, arguing that religion is an instrumental good for keeping the populace obedient to the laws and subservient to the state, but that the ruler operates by a different ethical code—that of preserving his throne and promoting the national interest.[17] In the contemporary era, realism tends to focus on power, competition, political actors, and material interests entirely devoid of ethical content.

Thus in practice, Western policies informed by the national interest and/or Western "values" may seem immoral, illegitimate, and blasphemous in highly religious contexts. Much like the liberal internationalists discussed earlier; in short, realist approaches that treat morality and religious faith as an entirely private matter—or a nonsensical, superstitious one—run the risk of not simply misunderstanding other societies, but also being viewed as immoral by those countries the United States is trying to engage. Likewise, security policies that attempt to pay off the victims of "collateral damage," making it simply an economic transaction rather than the venue for culturally relevant expressions of remorse and mourning, run the risk of not simply being callous but of being labeled as immoral. Western pressure on Muslim, Catholic, and Hindu societies to change laws regarding the family, divorce, maternal health, reproduction, abortion—perhaps understood by the West as levers to make these countries more Western, secular, and sophisticated—often result in backlashes against Washington as irreligious, Crusader-esque, and immoral.

At the same time, Western realists who are willing to promote human rights and liberties in one context (e.g., sub-Saharan Africa) but not others (e.g., northern Africa) due to political sensitivities favoring American interests are clearly seen as hypocrites by reformers, democrats, and the oppressed around the world. In other words, it is not religion itself that is the solution or the problem, it is realism's tendency to act consistently on behalf of U.S. material and security interests and therefore act inconsistently on behalf of the human rights and security of foreigners, drawing the moral approbation of religious and other skeptics of American intentions.

Realism need not be immoral or ethically hypocritical, but is often seen as such by others around the world. Foreign populaces, particularly religious and ethnic minorities suffering at the hands of authoritarian regimes, condemn American immorality for allying with regimes like those in Riyadh, Cairo, and Moscow while trumpeting liberty, democracy, and human rights in other venues. In contrast, a morally informed realism could, on the one hand, continue to assess the world in terms of power, interests, and self-help while recognizing the role of religious factors around the globe and pragmatically seeking a more consistent U.S. foreign policy on issues of democracy and human freedom.

Conclusion: Realism, Power, and Religion

When applied to contemporary U.S. foreign policy, the ideational superstructures of contemporary liberal internationalism and realism have failed to adequately account for many of the issues that religion brings to international politics, including questions of legitimate authority, power, interests, morality, and ethical consistency in foreign policy objectives. There is an alternative viewpoint in IR theory that can shed some light on the theoretical issues involved: constructivism. As discussed in Chapter 2, constructivism is emblematic of a "third Great Debate" in IR theory that seeks to "deconstruct" the presuppositions of the theory and get at the ideational underpinnings of existing political structures like anarchy, self-help, and the national interest. Where constructivism is most helpful is reminding foreign policy and culture experts that society's values and the national interest come from somewhere: they are generally deeply embedded in historical experience, culture, and religion. Therefore the state of international politics that is not immutable nor is it inevitable, it is simply "what states make of it."[18] The constructivist critique is useful in reminding social scientists and diplomats alike to seriously, and humbly, consider the future trajectory of international relations as well as the value assumptions that underlie the beliefs and behavior of states and citizenries. However, unlike liberalism and realism, constructivism's "deconstructive" approach has far less power in generating concrete foreign policy prescriptions and thus has not been a central feature of this book.

Constructivism has good news for realism and liberalism: change is possible in the world, and both perspectives can reach into their existing toolboxes to include analyses of religious factors in their foreign policy projects. As discussed above, realists can widen their analyses of power to include social, religious, and cultural forms of influence and authority—many of which have distinct implications for U.S. foreign policy in Iraq, Afghanistan, and elsewhere. Liberal internationalists can widen their understanding of evolving international norms as well as the role of nongovernmental actors to include faith-based understandings of human rights and a wider set of civil society partners, including religiously inspired NGOs and houses of worship. Both viewpoints must take into account the grating, offensive characteristics of Western secular approaches to development, military security, and pop culture that can result in serious blowback against the United States due to charges of hubris, hedonism, and hypocrisy. However, at present these approaches—including constructivism—tend to side together against the in-depth study of religious factors in IR theory, causing a fourth Great Debate as discussed in previous chapters. Nonetheless, realism and liberalism are uniquely suited to inclusion of religious variables in order to better explain the intersection of religion, war, and security in contemporary international affairs, which will have practical value in preventing misunderstanding, de-escalating conflict, and promoting peace.

CHAPTER 5

The Religious Dynamics of War and Peace

"Not one step back—Liberty or Death!" reads the black and red logo of Colombia's National Liberation Army (*Ejército de Liberación Nacional* [ELN]). Although less well-known than Colombia's more famous guerrilla army, the FARC, the ELN nonetheless is a thorn in the side of Colombia's government, responsible for nearly half of century of kidnappings, violence, and extortion. Unlike the secular-Marxist FARC and most other leftist Latin American movements, the ELN is unique in theological justifications for its insurgency.

The ELN was founded in the early 1960s, inspired by Castro's successful Cuban revolution, Third World anti-colonialism, Marxism, and Catholic social teaching. More specifically, the ELN's founding creed is rooted in what has come to be known as "liberation theology." Liberation theology is the perspective that there is a Christian imperative to upset the status quo on behalf of the poor and the oppressed: the "preferential option for the poor." Liberation theology emphasizes that in a fallen world epitomized by structural injustices, such as class structure and capitalism, Christians are enjoined to work on behalf of social justice, even if that means radical action. In the 1960s this nascent theology of liberation was fueled not only by the fall of colonial empires and militant socialism, but also by major changes in the Roman Catholic Church inaugurated during Vatican II (1962–65), which emphasized Church responsibility to the poor and making the Church more modern and accessible.

For much of its existence the vanguard of the ELN has been Catholic priests, most famously Father Camilo Torres Restrepo, a former university professor, who provided much of the theological rationale for the movement in its early years. Torres was killed fighting in 1966 but his memory has inspired a generation of priests and subsequent ELN leaders such as Spanish priest Father Manuel Perez who claim that Christ was a revolutionary fighting against oppression and therefore they have a moral obligation to follow his example: to be witnesses against corruption in Bogotá and in the institutional Church, and to fight on until all of Colombia is liberated from injustice, inequality, and poverty.[1] In doing so, the ELN has employed kidnapping, terrorism, and violence and financed itself through ransom, "protecting" oil pipelines (extortion), and most recently, drug sales.

Colombia has been a critical area of interest for the United States for the past 30 years, in part due to its influential cartels and the drug trade. But how is the United States to understand the complexities of the situation? Is Colombia just another developing country with a rural insurgency? Are the ideologies of the secular FARC and liberationist ELN important in the calculations of Bogotá and Washington? Are different approaches appropriate whether or not one is negotiating with secularists or religious adherents? How should the United States view Colombia's long-time right-wing paramilitary organizations, many of whom claim to be conservative Catholics? Moreover, can one understand a major Colombia politician, like recently retired President Álvaro Uribe, without considering his explicit, personal faith? How should we analyze the Colombian Catholic Church's peace initiatives, both those that have saved individual lives in specific places at specific times, and the on-again, off-again efforts to mediate an end to the conflict that typically end in the insurgents walking away from the table?

Colombia is just one reminder that that people around the world not only practice their faith through acts of veneration and worship, but also mobilize politically on the basis of ethnicity, nationalism, culture, and religion. Colombia is not alone in the western hemisphere when it comes to religiously informed violence, be it sectarian violence in southern Mexico over the past 20 years, the ongoing persecution of people of faith in Cuba and Venezuela, religious factionalism in Guatemala's horrific civil war, or the apocalyptic consequences of David Koresh. More broadly, religious dynamics (e.g., actors, worldviews, and cultures) infused numerous conflagrations in the 1990s including Bosnia, Rwanda, Afghanistan, and Sudan. This chapter considers how scholars and foreign policy experts should understand the diverse impulses of religious organizations and individuals on behalf of competition, bloodshed, reconciliation, and peace; presenting a descriptive model of *direct* and *indirect* ways that religious factors induce conflict or promote peace, with examples from across the globe.

International Relations Theory Explaining War

What has been lacking in IR theory's analysis of war and peace is thoughtful scholarship on how religious variables directly and indirectly cause or exacerbate conflict and how they can support or cause peace. Instead, traditional IR theory scholarship has focused on a variety of other factors of war, including the "three levels of analysis."[2] The first level of analysis is the individual level: how individual human beings directly cause or exacerbate conflict and the personal, psychological, and human nature explanations for war more generally. For instance, how can one understand World War II without understanding Adolf Hitler? How can one understand the Napoleonic wars without understanding Napoleon? How can one understand the rise to imperial greatness of Rome without thinking about the wars of Julius Caesar and his peers?

First-level analyses of the cause of war are focused on a variety of individual level factors. Thomas Hobbes, in *Leviathan*, observed, "In the nature of man, we find three principal causes of quarrel. First, competition; secondly, diffidence (fear); thirdly, glory."[3] Hobbes is speaking about the state of nature—man against man—but he generally assumes that relations between governments operate in a similar fashion. More generally, contemporary authors focusing on first-level explanations for conflict have focused on greed, hate, the so-called lust for power (*libidus dominandi*), and psychological dynamics, such as those of Alexander the Great, Genghis Khan, or Adolf Hitler.[4] It is true that to understand many conflicts, the decisions and decision-making processes made by key leaders matter, be they generals in war or political officials, but regrettably few recent studies evaluate the religious dimension of individual motivations.[5]

IR theory has also pointed us to a series of second level analysis factors, specifically, domestic politics. At the second level of analysis scholars ask the question, "How do domestic political factors, such as regime type and influential interest groups, affect the decision to go to war and how war is fought?" For example, it is well-documented that Japan's decision to declare war on the United States with an attack on Pearl Harbor in December 1941 was not made by a single person but through the bargaining between different elite factions: the military, the business class, and those close to the emperor. The policy outcome of this political "logrolling" was inherently shaped by the policy process itself.[6] Likewise, democratic peace theory argues that democracies are less likely to go to war—at least among themselves—and suggests that unstable and authoritarian regimes are much more likely, for a variety of reasons, to resort to force. Democratic peace theory's explanation is that the mechanisms for peace are checks and balances (separation of powers, popular opinion, critical role of an independent press) present in representative democracies, which make going to war difficult. In contrast, authoritarian regimes who can prop up their legitimacy by the "rally round the flag" effects and unstable governments in a major political transition (including democratic transition) are the most likely to go to war.[7] Rather than focusing heavily on second level explanations, the chapter will tease out where and when religious themes and actors directly or indirectly induce war or peace. It should be noted, however, that it is entirely possible for "religionized politics" to either provide the *raison d'être* of a state like Iran or the primary collective critique against the status quo like Egypt's Muslim Brotherhood.[8] In either case, religious actors, parties, and justifications underscore violence at home and against their neighbors.

IR theory has a third level of analysis identified by Kenneth Waltz's 1959 classic *Man, the State, and War*: the international system. Waltz argued that international politics is defined by anarchy: there is no central government to stop states from going to war. Waltz famously called anarchy the "permissive cause" of interstate war. In other words, the lack of centralized government authority means there is little to stop the next interstate war. The early twenty-first century is a globalized world with transnational networks, from the Roman Catholic Church to Facebook; and is characterized by global means of instantaneous communication, rapid and cheap international travel, increasingly shared sets of competing values at the international level, fungibility of economic assets, and the democratization of firepower (e.g., the legitimacy of democracy and human rights). Today it is not only states but other actors who compete, contend, cooperate, and challenge one another for resources and legitimacy in the global public sphere. All of these venues for competition can be points of contact for peace as well. At the international level, transnational religious actors like al Qaeda have perpetrated violence across the globe; transnational religious actors organize and invest in humanitarian and development programming, such as in the wake of Haiti's 2010 earthquake.

U.S. foreign policy should not dismiss religious factors in war as smokescreens for economic interests, nor should it make the mistake of believing that all religiously inspired warmongering or peacebuilding are alike. Religious factors, from divine revelation to the manipulation of religious symbols by political elites, share a religious intentionality in their justification for war or peace and are arguably the most powerful inducement for or against conflict in the world today, and therefore must be carefully analyzed by foreign policy and national security professionals.

Religious Factors and War

Religious variables have largely been left out of the traditional international relations scholarship, in part because they are ideational in nature rather than material. Much of the existing scholarship and policy analysis assumes that people and states go to war, or sue for peace, based solely on their material interests. Within the three levels of analysis, Western, secular, materialist explanations undergird much of IR theory on war: economic competition, the struggle for resources, the security dilemma, retaining the throne by relying on rally effects. These explanations of conflict are often useful, but they neglect the consideration of other distinct factors such as culture, religion, and ideology that may provide competing justifications for violence and/or may inform the definition of collective and individual interests. One way to see the nuances of religious factors is to distinguish *direct* and *indirect* pathways by which religion can inspire conflict and peace across the levels of analysis.

Direct Religious Factors

The first and most obvious way that religion can induce conflict is when a religious text or divine revelation directly mandates violence. To be more specific, if an individual or group receives a divine command to engage in violence, or if a religious text specifically commands that group to engage in violence, this is an example of religion directly causing conflict. Perhaps the best known historical example is the wars of the Old Testament in which the Hebrews were told specifically to act as agents of judgment upon their idolatrous neighbors: this was a direct revelation to Moses, Joshua, and others.

Today Joseph Kony, leader of the Lord's Resistance Army, which terrorizes northern Uganda and the tri-border region there (Sudan and Congo) provides a unique example of divine revelation. Joseph Kony has said on numerous occasions that the Holy Spirit speaks directly to him and tells him and tells him what to do: "They [spirits] speak to me. They load through me. They will tell us what is going to happen. They say 'you, Mr. Joseph, tell your people that the enemy is planning to come and attack.'"[9] On another occasion Kony asserted, "Yes, we are fighting for Ten Commandments. Is it bad? It is not against human rights. And that commandment was not given by Joseph (Kony). It was not given by the LRA. No, that commandment was given by God." Kony went on to explain that the LRA is "fighting for Uganda to be a free state governed by the Ten Commandments, a democratic state, and a state with a freely elected president."[10] It is beyond the scope of this chapter to examine the seeming disjuncture between the religious ideology of the LRA and its horrific tactics in the field (e.g., cutting off the ears, noses, and lips of children) or determine whether or not Kony and all of his senior lieutenants *continue* to believe that God is directing them—this has been a consistent mantra for over 20 years since the LRA's predecessor movement, Alice Auma's Holy Spirit Movement in the 1980s.[11] In sum, Kony and the LRA comprise a case of religious beliefs directly contributing to contemporary conflict. Interestingly, however, direct revelation is rare in the full range of warfare.

A second direct way that religion can induce conflict is when religious actors claim the authority to prescribe killing. In general this is when someone whose legitimacy and authority within their group is defined in terms of their religious knowledge and/or their religious position. Based on that status they tell their followers to engage in killing. This has been an element of Muqtada al-Sadr's legitimacy in Iraq: his family boasts a well-documented direct descent from the prophet Muhammad and he comes from a long line of influential clerics with vast influence in the region. His father, a well-known cleric, and two brothers were murdered (or martyred) by Saddam Hussein. Muqtada al-Sadr, although young and not a traditional ayatollah with the recognized authority to proclaim fatwas, nonetheless appropriated a religious and social bully pulpit based on religious authority. Al-Sadr consequently built the Mahdi Army as a "self-defense force" that has been very aggressive against Coalition forces, Sunnis, and rival Shia. Elsewhere, some Orthodox priests in the Bosnian wars of the early 1990s used their pulpit to prescribe violence against their enemies. This is precisely how Osama bin Laden, the founder of al Qaeda, behaved, claiming that contemporary Islam practiced in Saudi Arabia and elsewhere is corrupt and abominable. Although not a formal religious or political leader, bin Laden claimed that through his own study and personal piety he led a reformation within Islam, claiming authority within Islam. It is from this standpoint that he prescribed killing as a prophetic voice within the Islamic community.[12]

A third way that religion can directly induce violence is when those who are engaged in violence use religion to justify their claims. Often this is not a religious leader; it is the follower. Many suicide bombers are the rank-and-file members of their movement and have little formal religious training and no standing as religious authorities. Nonetheless, they cite religious justifications for their actions. These explanations are often religiously inspired , but lack a deep knowledge of theology, and hence are what Scott Appleby has called "weak religion." Weak religion is shallow and easily manipulable. Appleby argues that the theologically illiterate are the most likely to be motivated by simple theological justifications for violence such as a future in Paradise surrounded by dozens of willing virgins or religious arguments that nonbelievers are subhuman, demoniacal, or objects of divine wrath.[13]

Chilling evidence of this is available in a series of interviews by the Israeli government that documents the motivations of failed suicide bombers—those Palestinians who planned or tried to blow themselves up but failed to do so due to a faulty mechanism on the explosive or because they were captured at the last minute. These are not scholars of the Quran nor are they religious authorities. They do not claim a divine voice compelled their obedience to kill. They tend to be young men that often know little of the Quran. When asked about their reason for their participation in violence, they blend a variety of motives: the national "humiliation" of the Palestinian people, a sense that they have no hope and their lives are not going anywhere, heavenly rewards, and defense of Allah, the Quran, and the al-Aqsa Mosque (Dome of the Rock). In sum, they cite religion without theological sophistication, religious authority, or divine revelation, as one among many justifications for engaging in violence.

A fourth way that religion can directly exacerbate or cause conflict is when religion sacralizes a tangible thing or place, thereby making it holy and result-ing in a perceived obligation to protect that thing or place by religious adher-ence. A contemporary example of this can be found on the Indian subcontinent, infused by Islamist violence, Hindu nationalism (*hindutva*), and various local and regional flashpoints. Perhaps the most explosive was the 1992 destruction of the Babri mosque at Ayodhya in Uttar Pradesh by Hindu nationalists. The riot-ing that followed killed thousands and resulted in heightened tensions across the region.

What caused this eruption of violence? The sacred Hindu text *Ramayana* calls Ayodhya the birthplace of Lord Rama, one of Hinduism's most important gods, an incarnation of the god Vishnu.[14] Hindu nationalists claim that the site origi-nally housed a Hindu temple on the birthplace of Lord Rama that was destroyed in the early sixteenth century by the Muslim Emperor Babur, who built the Babri Mosque on the site. In 1992 not only was the site attacked by Hindu nationalists in order to liberate it from Muslims, but a national Hindu building campaign was initiated in which 300,000 bricks were sanctified from communities across India and then brought—often by foot—to Ayodhya to assist in the construction of a new temple.[15] It was only in late 2010 that the Indian judiciary ordered a legal resolution, mandating that the site be shared between Muslims and Hindus.[16] In short, the past 20 years have witnessed rioting, arson, and attacks on pilgrims venturing to this and other sacred places in India as both sides try to assert their claim to the site.

In the fall of 2010 a similar instance occurred when a previously unknown American Christian pastor claimed that he was going to burn copies of the Quran at his tiny church in Florida on September 11. Since the Quran is the primary holy text for Muslims, the provocative claim quickly went global thanks to the internet and a simultaneous controversy over the building of an Islamic center and mosque near Ground Zero in New York City. In the United States no one died or was injured, although the media frenzy was intense. In contrast, in Muslim-majority countries around the world, dozens of people died in rioting sparked by the Florida provocation. What were they rioting about? What caused the violence? Muslims responded to the affront with great vigor and violence as a demonstration of the need to protect the holy Quran.

Indirect Religious Factors

Consequently, there are at least four ways that religious actors and themes directly induce or exacerbate conflict: divine revelation, religious authority, religious justifications, and sacralization. These factors tend to explicate elements of conflict at the individual or the collective level—in other words, at the first or second levels of analysis. There are less direct ways that religion can cause or exacerbate conflict, either in terms of social identity or manipulation of religious symbols.

The first and, generally the most potent, indirect form of religion inspiring violence is when faith identification serves as a critical social identity marker and cleavage point for political competition or for competition for economic resources. Again, religion can exacerbate conflict when it is essential to the formation of sectarian identity. Most "religious wars" are precisely this: battles between groups who self-identify along cultural, ethnic, and religious lines and see others as rivals.

For example, in Lebanon over the past half century there has been a number of bloody wars, all infused to some extent with religious overtones. The antagonists in each of these conflicts self-identify and have been identified by their challengers by their religious heritage: Shia Muslims, Druze, Maronite and other Christians, Sunni, and a variety of other groups in between. What the media tends to report is Muslims killing Christians, Christians killing Muslims, attacks on and by the Jewish state, and so on. But the conflict has nothing to do with who the Orthodox patriarch is, who the Catholic prelate is, or the theologies of the Quran, Torah, or Bible. What is being disputed is not faith, nor theology, nor sacred sites. Rather, the contest is for patronage, access to power, economic resources, and political privilege. In Lebanon, religion is a critical marker to distinguish "us" versus "them"—"us" Christians versus "those" Druze, "us" Shia versus "those" Christians, and the like. Were the Lebanese model to take the global stage, as suggested by Samuel Huntington's *The Clash of Civilizations*, the world is in for a debilitating inter-civilizational struggle. Philip Jenkins, author of *The Next Christendom*, says,

> My nightmare, looking at some of these figures, is that the next Christendom might also be the age of the next crusade and the next jihad—somewhat different from the thirteenth century, in that it will be fought with much more

high-tech weapons. The thought of the power balance of the thirteenth century armed with nuclear weapons and anthrax is not a pleasant one.[17]

This is similar to what happened in Northern Ireland in the conflict between Catholics and Protestants. Northern Ireland has a long history of difference and discrimination, but no one there was fighting over the number of books in the Bible, about theology, about the nature of communion, about the infallibility of the pope, or any of these things on which Catholics and Protestants do differ. Instead, the "Troubles" that have lasted for the better part of three decades, was and is a conflict about discrimination, economic and political opportunity, nationalism, crime, and rights. Over time, the conflict devolved into tit-for-tat violence by groups who identified as religious but where religion was not the driving factor.

Indeed, the principle group on the Catholic side in Northern Ireland, the Irish Republican Army (IRA) and its political wing Sinn Féin, are not religious entities although supposedly defending Catholicism. The IRA judged the institutional Catholic Church to be taking a quietistic role, keeping its head in the sand and supporting the status quo. In contrast, the IRA and Sinn Féin's intellectual roots are in a left-of-center, secularist twentieth-century nationalism rather than in the ideology of a Catholic-inspired insurgency like Colombia's ELN.[18]

A second way that religious variables can indirectly contribute to conflict is when religious symbols are manipulated for sectarian or mass mobilization and thus they become collective action frames. In other words, when elites (political or religious) instrumentalize religious symbols as political objects, or the citizenry rally behind a symbol, a color, a date, a place; this mobilization is a way that religion can become an indirect symbol influencing conflict.

Bosnia provides an example of how these indirect trends of communal identity and elite manipulation of religious symbols induce and exacerbate conflict. Although Cold War Yugoslavia carefully instituted comprehensive programs to develop a national identity, as late as 1988 only six percent of the populace self-identified first as a "Yugoslav."[19] Conversely, when asked which nationality they identify with, 77 percent of Orthodox Christians identified as Serbs, 82 percent of Muslims as Albanians, and 89 percent of Croats as Catholic. When asked to identify the "other" as having a synonymous religious and national identity, majorities of all groups agreed that it means the same thing to be Serb and Orthodox, Croat and Catholic, and Albanian and Muslim. Interestingly, when asked if they consider themselves to be religious, Croats responded "yes" 56 percent of the time compared to 37 percent for Muslims but less than 19 percent for Serbs.

Despite only a fraction of the population claiming to be religious, Serbian nationalists, including Orthodox religious leaders, used religious imagery and claims in the 1990s to justify Serb aggression. Although it is true that the disintegration of Yugoslavia was rooted in the economic and political failure of Yugoslavia and pan-Europe Communism more generally, ethnoreligious identity was key for mobilizing constituencies and defining the enemy. For example, a prominent Serbian political scientist at Belgrade University asserted in 1991,

> Balkan Muslims have the blood of martyrs of Kosovo on their hands...international Islamic planners, aided by domestic fellow-thinkers, have as their objective to Islamize all of Serbia, but only as the first step of a breakthrough into Europe...Islam is an enemy religion today, as it was yesterday.[20]

Politicians and religious leaders used churches and crypts as the venue for political rallies; Crusader crosses began to pop up on clothing, billboards, and graffiti; martial music from an earlier era—venerating the Fatherland and the sacrificial death of the warrior—found its way into the airwaves. Despite the low level of religiosity of much of the populace, during the conflict this religious mobilization and identification engulfed hundreds of thousands of people, reminiscent of how a millennium earlier, the Crusaders used the cross—and Muslims the crescent—to raise armies, as battle flags for warfare, and to symbolize calls by both armies for the liberation of sacred places.

Religious Factors for Peace

Religious factors can directly induce or exacerbate violence; they can also support or contribute to peace directly or indirectly. First, religion can directly contribute to peace when an individual or group renounces violence based on a (direct) religious text, personal spiritual encounter, or revelation. Thus, some Christians reading the Gospel of Mathew and Jesus' injunction, "Turn the other cheek" make a commitment to pacifism and nonviolence.[21] Pacifists and advocates of nonviolence come in many different forms, from those who entirely eschew any conflict (conscientious objectors and peace protestors) to those who are willing to provide aid to the needy and wounded—even on the battlefield (some Quakers)—to some Catholics who have been heavily engaged in peacebuilding in Central America and Colombia. A second, parallel way that religion may directly contribute to peace is when an individual or a group reports a calling or vocation to engage in faith-inspired peacemaking. Particularly since the Vietnam era, the Mennonites have affirmed such a calling. One example was the partnership of Mennonite conflict resolution expert John Paul Lederach with local churches and international religious groups to facilitate meetings between the Sandinista regime and indigenous groups from Nicaragua's East Coast. A series of difficult meetings in 1987–1988 established communication between the belligerents, ultimately undergirding a 1989 peace deal.[22] Similarly, over the past 200 years, Quaker organizations have reported a calling to peace, moving beyond conscientious objection to assisting the vulnerable or to working on behalf of peace.[23]

An example of a religious group blending several of these approaches is Community Sant'Egidio, a Catholic lay organization based in Rome. Beginning in the early 1980s Sant'Egidio began to engage—quietly—with leaders on both sides of Mozambique's long and bloody civil war. On the one hand was the government known as FRELIMO (Frelimo), originally claiming a Marxist ideology and with various external supporters; and on the other hand were the rebels (RENAMO), supported by South Africa and other outside partners. Sant'Egidio built personal relationships with leaders on both sides while providing humanitarian and development assistance, free of charge, to people on both sides. In short, the Community acted in a spirit of peace to alleviate suffering in a conflict zone. Over time, Sant'Egidio built informal, but strong, relationships with both sides of the conflict allowing them to host informal meetings between the antagonists in the late 1980s. Ultimately Sant'Egidio led in brokering the peace deal (1992) that ended Mozambique's civil war. In the ceremony marking the signing of the peace agreement, the representatives of Sant'Egidio specifically spoke of reconciliation transforming opponents into "brothers and sisters in Christ."[24]

Third, religion can contribute directly to peace when religious elites use their spiritual authority to act as agents of peace. More specifically, this is when a religious actor whose legitimacy and social authority is rooted in their religious tradition, in their position within the religious hierarchy, or in their distinctive religious service. Perhaps the most famous example of this in recent times is Archbishop Desmond Tutu, who fought nonviolently against the apartheid system of South Africa from an overtly Christian perspective, earning him the Nobel Peace Prize.[25] There were alternatives to the nonviolent "religious militancy for peace" that Tutu and his allies practiced,[26] including the African National Congress (ANC), which took a secular-, nationalist-, and Marxist-inspired approach to fighting against apartheid. The ANC and other groups responded, on occasion, to apartheid with violence but Tutu and many of the black churches took a parallel, but different, track to criticizing the structural violence of South African society and building alliances for social justice. They did so, in part, by using their bully pulpits on behalf of peace.

Furthermore, it is hard to imagine the South African miracle occurring without the inspirational leadership of individuals, religious or not, like Tutu and Nelson Mandela. Tutu was instrumental in the transition phase as a key leader in South Africa's Truth and Reconciliation Commission (TRC), which openly engaged raw issues of truth, justice, and mercy from a perspective informed by religion. The TRC was not religious per se, but one cannot understand its fundamental principles without some sense of the Christian theology and local cultural principles (e.g., *ubuntu*'s emphasis on collective identity and responsibility) inherent to it, nor can one dismiss the role of prayer and clergy commissioners, as well as the overt support from black and white churches for the TRC.

The TRC suggests a fourth way that religious factors can contribute to peace. Religiously inspired claims can redefine divisive social identities to promote reconciliation. This process, albeit difficult and rare, relies on religious teaching, spiritual insight, and conflict resolution techniques to transform former opponents to God's children, changing one's enemies to one's brothers and sisters. This redefinition can be used by religious peacemakers to redefine the identities of former combatants.

In such instances, religious people often first have to seek conciliation among competing faith traditions and then broaden that engagement on the national political stage. A case in point is the ecumenical women's movement in Liberia that erupted onto the national scene during Liberia's second civil war (1999–2003). At the time, the regime of President Charles Taylor was in a terrible conflict against rebel forces operating under the rubric Liberians United for Reconciliation and Democracy (LURD). Both sides were guilty of atrocities, following a pattern set in Liberia's first civil war that brought Taylor to power early in the 1990s, including organized mass rape, maimings, the destruction of civilian homes and villages, and extrajudicial murders. By 2003 Liberia was a country decimated economically, politically, psychologically, and spiritually.[27]

In April 2003 a new women's organization was formed, inspired by a Lutheran woman named Leymeh Gbowee: the Women in Peacebuilding Network. Gbowee and some friends began by meeting for prayer and consultation with other Christians but within months other groups joined the effort, such as the Liberian Women's Initiative and the Mano River Union Peace Network. Most importantly, in a society that has large Christian and Muslim populations, the Women in Peacebuilding Network early on sought out Muslim women and their imams as partners in an effort to bring peace to their country.[28]

The peacebuilding efforts of the Women in Peacebuilding Network were captured on international television, including the BBC and other major outlets, as they held prayer vigils on the main highway to the Monrovia airport.[29] Regional leaders were amazed to see the mass uprising of women of various faith groups, united in calls for national reconciliation. Ultimately, the political climate forced President Taylor to directly accept a peace document on behalf of this faith-inspired group of mothers and wives. Moreover, when the Economic Community of West African States (ECOWAS) led peace talks in neighboring Accra, women from the Peacebuilding Network not only attended the meetings, but captured the attention of the international community by barricading the antagonists in the building so that a peace deal would be signed. All of these efforts began and were infused with overt theological themes of violence as sin, the need for repentance and forgiveness, the theological imperatives of loving one's neighbor, and the possibilities of transcendent reconciliation in tandem with prayer, singing, and testimonials.[30] Today, their postconflict work continues, aiding in the demobilization and reintegration of ex-combatants and emphasizing forgiveness.

Finally, religion may contribute to peace when faith-inspired forgiveness transcends the often-unresolved issues of a conflict. Of course, this is extremely difficult to work out in practice, especially in interstate war. Nonetheless, forgiveness is a transcendent opportunity for individuals to move beyond the past legacy of violence.

Many political systems have attempted to approximate this over the past 20 years, learning lessons about political forgiveness, amnesty, truth seeking, political reconciliation, and justice in Latin America and sub-Saharan Africa. From an institutional perspective, faith-inspired forgiveness is difficult to employ on behalf of governments, yet there is the testimony of thousands of people who indicated that their faith inspired them to forgive people who have stolen from them, who killed their loved ones, and who harmed their lives in places like Colombia and Rwanda.

At the collective level, this has been implemented in some cases by approximating justice and forgiveness through transitional justice and truth and reconciliation commissions. These commissions often record and document the experience of victims and the crimes of perpetrators and symbolically, at a collective political level, offer an accounting and an opportunity for regret and social forgiveness. Often when these work there are strong elements of religious faith, be it prayers by clerics or the inclusion of religious leaders on the tribunals, such as happened in South Africa and East Timor. In many cases, successful commissions include religious practices or culturally appropriate practices (with religious components), such as Muslim countries' *shura*, *sulh*, and *jirga*, East Timor's *naha bitte boot*, Rwanda's *gacaca* courts, Bangladesh's *shalish*, and Botswana's *kgotla*.[31]

Scholars of Islam suggest that such practices can help ameliorate conflict in the Middle East and Central Asia. More specifically, from the time of Mohammed,

Islam has had a tradition of arbitration and reconciliation, both internally and with non-Muslims: *sulh*. Mohammed (at times) sought peaceful accommodation with his Jewish and Christian neighbors and the fourth caliph—Ali—accepted arbitration (*tahkim*) with the governor of Syria over the objections of many of his hard-line supporters. The Quran and many jurists emphasize the importance of *sulh* as a binding contract for peace.[32] Muslims historically signed treaties with numerous non-Muslim neighbors, including Syria, Armenia, Cyprus, and Sudan.[33] UCLA expert Khaled Abou El Fadl argues:

> Muslim jurists regularly cited the arbitration precedent in support of the desirability of negotiated settlements in political, commercial, and personal disputes. Although the arbitration incident sheds little light on recommended parameters of compromise, it does help to establish the normative value of compromise in Islamic political and legal discourse.[34]

What of those who refuse to participate in efforts to resolve the conflict? According to El Fadl, the Quran (49:9) calls such people "transgressors" for violating the need for peace, and they are to be fought against:

> If two parties among the believers fall into a quarrel, make peace between them. But if one of the parties transgresses against the other, then fight all against the transgressor until it complies with God's command. If it complies, then make peace between them with justice and fairness.[35]

Furthermore, according to El Fadl, Islam does have a tradition of dealing with Muslim secessionists and rebels. If the rebels' underlying motivation is principled (*ta'wil*), "the rebels [were] to be treated leniently...they acquired a protected status known as *bughah*." Such rebels operated from an authentic normative commitment, not for the sake of violence itself, greed, kin- or tribal affiliation. El Fadl argues that conflict resolution—rather than battlefield domination or extermination—is the appropriate step with such rebels, providing them with a forum to air their grievances and attempting to reconcile them peacefully. Moreover, defeated rebels could not be "executed, tortured, or imprisoned" or lose their properties, but had to be reconciled to the community.[36]

Conclusion

In conclusion, the world is a highly religious place where communal identity, individual faith, and global religious movements cannot be separated from issues of governance, development, politics, or security. Few wars are directly, and solely, caused by religious reasons; but many of the past generation's conflicts have included differences of religious and ethnic identity, religious justifications for violence, and religious actors sanctioning efforts for war or peace. When religious identity and sacred issues are part of a wider set of dividing trends, such as economic grievance and human rights abuses, the mix can be nothing short of holy war waged on behalf of Serbian Orthodoxy, Islamic jihad, or insurgents like the LRA and ELN. But religious actors, themes, and practices can also provide the resources for diminishing difference, inspiring conflict resolution, and transcending past hurts to build a more secure peace. In the end, religious explanations tend to operate at the individual and collective levels of analysis, meaning that individuals, groups, and congregations are the key actors in promoting violence or peace and thus should be the focus for future study of the intersection of religion, war, and peace. The question is how can U.S. foreign policy best do this: sharpen its wits to consider religious trends in war and peace, develop a heightened awareness of religious dynamics in its diplomatic corps and military, and thoughtfully partner with religious actors, when appropriate, on behalf of security, peace, and justice? Part of the answer is to invest in religious literacy and government capacity.

CHAPTER 6

Enhancing U.S. Foreign Policy with
Religious Literacy

During the late 1980s, the U.S. ambassador to Liberia attempted to find channels for influencing Liberia's increasingly erratic President Samuel Doe. "Sergeant Doe," a member of the minority Krahn ethnic group, had led the 1980 coup d'état that overthrew the former government that had been run by members of the Americo-Liberian upper class for the 130 years since former American slaves founded Liberia. Doe and his henchmen killed or exiled much of the former ruling class in the aftermath of 1980, but took a strong pro-American (and anti-Soviet) stance and promised open elections in 1985. Not surprisingly, international observers declared the elections fraudulent, and the second half of Doe's rule focused more and more on stifling dissent through imprisonment, torture, and extrajudicial killing. One of the most famous of Doe's targets later became Liberia's president, Ellen Johnson-Sirleaf, who was imprisoned and exiled at various points of Doe's tenure.

How could the U.S. ambassador influence the regime on behalf of human rights and political reform as the Cold War and U.S. financial support was waning and President Doe was becoming more paranoid, unpopular, and repressive? Ambassador Edward Perkins, a career diplomat, discovered that although Liberia was a majority-Christian society, Doe's personnel spiritual advisor was a Muslim imam. Perkins engaged the imam in an untraditional effort at private diplomacy to gain the release of Ellen Johnson-Sirleaf and other political prisoners. The spiritual advisor agreed to a private meeting with the U.S. ambassador, handed him a Quran, and set simple rules for ongoing dialogue: the basis for his counsel to the Liberian president was the Quran. Hence, if the United States wanted to emphasize human rights or other policies, the imam would only listen if the message was rooted in the Quran. Perkins began reading. This outreach and subsequent carefully crafted arguments rooted in part in Islamic notions of humanity's value as the children of Allah, set the stage for an ongoing dialogue in which the U.S. ambassador targeted the Doe's human rights record through the language of the Quran.[1]

According to Perkins' autobiography, little in his professional training as a career diplomat prepared him to engage an imam through the Quran as a strategic focal point for furthering U.S. foreign policy objectives. In this case, the ambassador's personal religious faith made him sensitive to the importance of religious arguments across cultures. At the crucial moment, the embassy team had to quickly become literate in some Islamic fundamental premises; Islam had not previously received comparable attention as Liberian economics, development, and other sectors.

It is this awareness of religion and the need for religious literacy which is the focus of this and the two subsequent chapters. This chapter argues broadly that America needs a twenty-first century diplomacy that is religiously literate, just as the United States needs foreign policy expertise in economics, development, political-military affairs, and other avenues of U.S. foreign policy engagement. The biggest barrier to a religiously literate foreign policy, a "New Diplomacy," is the institutionalized nature of the "Old Diplomacy's" secularist biases, narrow focus on government-to-government engagement, and focus on traditional elements of national power. What the U.S. government must do to succeed in the New Diplomacy appropriate for a highly religious world is to clarify the appropriate domain for engaging religious factors in U.S. foreign policy, expand the knowledge resources available to foreign affairs specialists, invest in an improved array of assets and capabilities, and implement a political strategy for U.S. foreign policy in highly religious contexts.

Old vs. New Diplomacy: Adding Religious Literacy

The Old Diplomacy

U.S. history books portray diplomats as Ivy-leaguers sitting at foreign posts, building rapport with host-country elites at state dinners and galas, interacting strictly on a government-to-government basis, and narrowly focusing on the high politics of political competition and military security. This portraits smells of powdered wigs and dusty parchment, and thus is something of a caricature. What is true, however, is that many who represent the United States abroad are intelligent graduates of top American universities who work hard to build relationships with host-country government officials via social engagements and government-to-government meetings. Moreover, in many smaller foreign capitals, the U.S. delegation consists of just a handful to a dozen U.S. citizens assisted by a cadre of locals recruited as translators, workers, and critical intermediaries: "foreign service nationals."

Sometimes the presuppositions of such an approach are a legacy from the past. Old Diplomats were trained in theories of economics, law, and government.

This training was largely secular, underpinned by many of the secularist and modernization assumptions discussed previously. Old Diplomacy was largely government-to-government because it was assumed that the host government was the legitimate representative of the public it ostensibly served. Old Diplomacy venerated an extremely rigorous application of sovereignty, defined chiefly in terms of non-intervention in the affairs of another country, even in times of crisis or criminality. Hence, and despite many specific exceptions, U.S. government officials did not develop meaningful knowledge of or relationships with other social actors such as clerics, tribal leaders, democracy activists and the like.

Old Diplomacy tended to focus almost exclusively on "the national interest," defined in materialist terms of security and trade."[2] Old Diplomacy was jealously guided, and guarded, by the State Department; today there are approximately 6,000 Foreign Service officers at home and in approximately 175 countries abroad. Perhaps more importantly, Old Diplomacy meant that U.S. government agencies "stayed in their lanes": as a result, the State Department handled government-to-government relations, the military did traditional security work, the Treasury focused on finance, and USAID completed development work. Many vestiges of this compartmentalized situation still exist, such as the sometimes-awkward hierarchies and lines of authority between diplomats and defense attachés in foreign posts. A U.S. defense attaché—a colonel—at a U.S. posting declared unequivocally, "I do *not* work for the ambassador."

Under the norms of Old Diplomacy, the U.S. government provided services or funding to a foreign government directly. Old Diplomacy had few partners outside government service, although business interests were often consulted, particularly with opportunities and equities in the western hemisphere and the developing world. However, all of this is not to say that the Old Diplomacy was a failure. As Walter Russell Mead argues in his best-selling *Special Providence*, although pre-Cold War America is often castigated for not having a foreign policy, its foreign policy in its first century and a half was highly successful. The fledgling republic not only expanded and matured at home, but it successfully backed down the mighty British Empire on a number of occasions after the War of 1812, deployed the Marines from the "halls of Montezuma to the shores of Tripoli" on behalf of U.S. interests, beat the Spanish empire, balanced competing European interests and intrigues, avoided entanglement in a major European war for over a century, and spread American commercial interests around the world. Mead is right that there is much to credit in America's pre-World War II foreign policies. In the same way, there is much to credit in American leadership during the Cold War, including beating the Nazis but restoring Germany and Japan, creating a new world order and the Western alliance, containing and ultimately crippling the Soviet bloc, and seeing America's commercial interests and national prosperity become and remain the envy of the world.

Much has changed. Many of the elements of the post-Cold War world that are collectively called "globalization" have fundamentally altered the environment in which diplomacy takes place. The contemporary era is no longer defined by rigid government hierarchies, the lack of access to information, the slow movement of data and communications, expensive (in time and money) foreign travel, and strict national and cultural boundaries. Instead, the globalized world now includes major nongovernmental figures and organizations that have regional and even transnational constituencies; easy and plentiful access to information and intelligence; instantaneous transfers of data, communications, and finance; rapid and cheap travel without the boundaries of Cold War "curtains;" as well as competing and overlapping cultural, religious, national, and ethnic identities. No longer can U.S. foreign policy only focus on government-to-government relations; no longer is the U.S. government alone in promoting America's interests, ideals, and image. It is this globalized, energetic, culturally and religiously rich world that U.S. foreign policy faces, and it must keep the best of the Old Diplomacy and weave it with elements of New Diplomacy for the twenty-first century.

The New Diplomacy

The New Diplomacy builds on the strengths of U.S. diplomacy, integrates recent novel trends, and must expand and adapt new ways of understanding and behaving in the twenty-first century world. This book is not the first to call for new approaches to diplomacy—former Secretary of State Condoleezza Rice articulated a "transformational diplomacy" several years ago. Several elements of Secretary Rice's five-point "transformational diplomacy" initiative did not seem, at the time or now, to be paradigm shifting. She relocated diplomats from some embassies (e.g., Western Europe) to the capitals of rising powers such as China, India, and Brazil; required diplomats to serve in hardship posts and work with foreign partners to wean them from dependence on U.S. handouts. These all seem to be consonant with ongoing U.S. objectives, but not revolutionary changes. However, her initiative did call for increased language proficiency in the Foreign Service, which is congruent with the emphasis on relationships, culture, and religion in this book. Some of the first steps toward evolving U.S. diplomacy in a new century supported Bush Administration initiatives, particularly in empowering domestic and international faith-based organizations and rethinking some elements of public diplomacy. Most of Secretary Rice's innovations have continued under the new Administration; however, Secretary Clinton has spoken on numerous occasions about a "smart diplomacy" that is characterized by "international partnerships." Such partnerships, for instance with civil society actors as called for in the QDDR, including religious groups, are a change for many sectors of the U.S. foreign policy establishment outside the humanitarian and development community. However, there is little evidence at this writing—2 years into the Administration—of any substantive change on these issues.

This is not to say that there has been a transformation in how U.S. policymakers think about and engage the world, but that there has been some a growing awareness in some quarters of the Bush and Obama Administrations that U.S. diplomacy must evolve. Nonetheless, New Diplomacy goes much further: it assumes a richer, deeper world in which factors in addition to the national interest are important for developing the next cadre of foreign policy experts. Critical to such studies is the inclusion of material on religion and culture so that the next generation of U.S. government representatives have knowledge of the profound trends in contemporary world affairs and how America can engage on religious issues. This aligns with a recommendation by former Secretary of State Madeline Albright in her book, *The Mighty and the Almighty*:

> In the future, no American ambassador should be assigned to a country where religious feelings are strong unless he or she has a deep understanding of the faiths commonly practiced there. Ambassadors and their representatives, wherever they are assigned, should establish relationships with local religious leaders. The State Department should hire or train a core of specialists in religion to be deployed both in Washington and in key embassies overseas.[3]

In 2011 Douglas Johnston, reflecting on a similar argument made in his 1994 book *Religion, the Missing Dimension of Statecraft* said,

> Because fifteen years have passed since [publication] with next to nothing of an institutional nature done to fill this gap, one can only surmise that either the will to do so or the knowledge of how to do so (or perhaps both) is missing.[4]

What is needed is what Stephen Prothero calls "religious literacy." Prothero borrows the term, and its implications, from E. D. Hirsch's "cultural literacy": the core knowledge that literate citizens sharing a society need in order to be able to communicate with one another. Hirsch's notion of cultural literacy included names, dates, places, and phrases that were part of the shared lexicon—literally and metaphorically—of Americans, from "Remember the Alamo" to "your work was a homerun (or grand slam)!"

Prothero applied the idea to knowledge of basic doctrine and narratives of religion, arguing that Americans once had, and need again, an awareness of religious ideas and symbols. More specifically, "religious literacy refers to the ability to understand and use in one's day-to-day life the basic building blocks of religious traditions—their key terms, doctrines, symbols, sayings, characters, metaphors, and narratives."[5] Prothero concedes that it is probably better to speak of "religious literacies" due to the multidimensionality of global religion, but particularly at home in the United States, a basic knowledge of Christian ideas (due to American history) and other major faiths (due to growing diversity in a globalized world) is critical. By extension, those working with and living in other societies will need a basic religious and cultural literacy in order to build relationships and understand their surroundings.

New Diplomacy recognizes that in addition to currying relationships with foreign governments, the United States must likewise engage foreign publics. The United States began to do so a generation ago by helping others through efforts like the Peace Corps and USAID. However, there has always been tension about whether such assistance was philanthropic in nature or an instrument of national soft power. New Diplomacy is a broader engagement strategy that takes into account the real centers of power and authority within a society, not simply the elites in the capital. The United States found that neglecting such centers of authority, as in the case of Grand Ayatollah Ali Sistani in Iraq, can be detrimental to its interests. Fortunately, some U.S. foreign policy practitioners are implementing such strategies in highly religious societies. Examples include hosting and visiting Muslim and Christian leaders for meals and by holding *Iftar* dinners at U.S. embassies during Ramadan. At present such activities are ad hoc, dependent on the creativity and willingness of an ambassador or chargé d'affaires to consider alternate structures of legitimacy in a society. Those structures often tend to be religious and should be on the U.S. government's policy "map" as partners.

New Diplomacy respects sovereignty, but believes sovereignty rests in the people, and hence the New Diplomat reaches out across the spectra of society, especially to the lovers of freedom and champions of democracy. Late in the Clinton presidency and again during the Bush Administration, embassies were charged with reaching out to proponents of religious freedom and to democratic activists. New Diplomacy is thus interested in and attempts to become aware of the full range of religious and cultural factors pulsing through a society because such elements may contain the seeds for future conflict or the promise of peace. Ignoring them is simply not an option.

The Obama Administration seems to have realized this. In announcing the reorganized White House Office of Faith-Based and Neighborhood Partnerships, four goals were asserted, which included working with the National Security Council to foster interfaith dialogue with world leaders and scholars.[6] This suggests that some senior leaders recognize the strategic necessity of engaging faith leaders on issues of major import and that the United States should embrace its historical role as peacemaker by fostering interreligious dialogue.

New Diplomacy is an interagency, whole-of-government approach that recognizes that the persistent problems that most countries face are multidimensional in character and thus necessitate a multidimensional response from the United States. The conflicts in Darfur and northern Nigeria are cases in point, where disputes over land usage between groups are complicated by cultural and religious identities, creating intractable sectarian violence between communities. Recognizing the needs of the New Diplomacy, Gates testified to the U.S. Congress and asked for additional funding for the State Department and USAID, recognizing the needs for a multidimensional approach to America's engagement in the world. That engagement should include religious literacy for those serving in countries where the population is highly religious.

Old Diplomacy was about the national interest, often defined solely in terms of hard power. New Diplomacy has redefined American interests over the past 20 years to include normative and quality-of-life issues for foreign publics, most notably socio-economic development, human rights, and democracy promotion. New Diplomacy recognizes that human rights and democracy are rooted in normative values often associated with religion, and that religious actors can be key partners in advancing economic development goals and championing human rights and civil liberties. President Obama made this argument in his June 2009 Cairo speech, in which he explicitly asserted the links between women's rights, religious freedom and human rights, economic development (including entrepreneurship and the rule of law), and educational opportunity.

A positive trend in the evolution of New Diplomacy is the return of "public diplomacy." Public diplomacy is what (and how) the government communicates America's identity, values, and activities to foreign publics. In order to do public diplomacy well, as discussed later in this chapter, it is important that religious actors and communities are a part of the engagement strategy and that U.S. government messages are culturally relevant to foreign publics. This includes appreciating the deep values and sentiments of other nations, particularly those whose identities and social structures are infused with religion.

Four Recommendations for U.S. Foreign Policy

Clarify the Domain

How can the United States begin to implement the New Diplomacy, one that is religiously literate and sensitive to the religious and cultural dynamics of contemporary world affairs? Perhaps the most important step is for senior leaders to clarify the appropriate domain within which engaging religion is appropriate. Chapters 3 and 4 argued that, among other reasons, U.S. government workers resist engaging religious factors due to a deep uncertainty, and even fear, about its constitutionality and what it might do to their careers. This is not an unjustified phobia. A recent seminar for foreign policy officials in Washington, D.C. included five PowerPoint slides. The purpose of the presentation was to assert the potential and benefits of working with religious development actors overseas. However, the final slide was titled "Remember the Establishment Clause" and featured a photo of human hands clutching prison bars. This was an arresting image, and many in the seminar visibly sat back in their seats and folded their arms in what seemed to be the body language of, "I knew it...better to be safe and sorry...don't touch religion!" This is a chilling message, particularly for younger members of the Foreign Service, and one that is inconsistent with smart foreign policy as well as American jurisprudence.

Thus, senior leaders at the White House and Cabinet need to provide leadership and clarity to foreign affairs officials on the appropriate domain and boundaries of engaging religious actors and dynamics in U.S. foreign policy. Because the United States is embedded in the global resurgence of religion, the parameters of that domain should be quite expansive.

What is the fundamental dilemma? The essential issue at hand is whether the U.S. government, particularly when it engages or provides funding to nongovernmental entities, violates the First Amendment to the Constitution that there "shall be no establishment of religion." One aspect of the problem is misunderstanding or lack of knowledge by working-level officials about what U.S. policy allows and restricts when it comes to engaging religious actors. The problem is exacerbated when conflated with domestic culture wars that often have no bearing whatsoever on foreign policy: prayer before high school football games or menorahs and crèches at public libraries. This apprehension is also caused by a lack of leadership by senior officials, a sense that there is little political "cover" for engaging religious actors and situations, and a lack of clear, consistent guidance on the issues across the institutions of the U.S. government.

How can senior leaders clarify the domain? First, a statement by the president or secretary of state recognizing the global resurgence of religion and stating American intent to address the religious dimensions of statecraft would be helpful and appropriate. In many ways it seemed as if Obama's June 2009 Cairo speech, "A New Beginning," was just such a speech in its emphasis on the importance of religious liberty and the religious character of the United States and the Muslim world. However, to date it is unclear whether the speech had much policy traction within the agencies; nor have there been additional, complementary expressions by the vice president, secretary of state, or other senior officials.

In addition, the U.S. government should provide simple, direct guidance to departments and agencies on the appropriate domain for such engagement in U.S. foreign policy. The executive branch has tremendous latitude when it comes to foreign policy, particularly when it comes to national security, defense, and intelligence. Hence, it is likely that the general application of "boundaries" will primarily apply to direct government funding to religious actors in civil society, such as religiously inspired development and humanitarian organizations. Fortunately, there already exists excellent, unambiguous guidance on this topic—USAID's Bush-era guidelines for funding faith-based organizations. The USAID guidelines, documented in Chapter 7, offer plain-spoken, direct counsel based on common sense and U.S. law and are a model for an interagency approach to these issues; or at least they were until the Obama Administration removed them from public view.[7] A common-sense conclusion drawn from USAID's guidance and recent Supreme Court decisions is that whereas the U.S. government has wide latitude to engage and even provide direct financial support to religious organizations when they are engaged in nonsectarian work (e.g., providing humanitarian assistance, development aid, job training, etc.), there is no justification to sustain a program that is out of line with American values and its society or which has proselytism as its primary activity.

In theory, the U.S. government would make the work of foreign assistance much easier if standardized, simple guidelines such as those of USAID were utilized across the board and if each and every case did not have to run a seemingly endless yet inconsistent gauntlet of internal legal opinion. However, the actuality in practice is quite difficult. Even with guidelines like those of USAID, the internal mechanisms of USAID, State, and other departments move cautiously and glacially. Programs and grants that involve faith-based actors often run lengthy reviews through multiple sets of in-house lawyers, without consistency across bureaus and offices. In short, high-level guidance, such as a directive from the White House and/or the Justice Department's Office of Legal Counsel is needed.

Moreover, as noted earlier, thoughtful leaders within agencies should make it clear that smart diplomacy does not limit U.S. government officials from building enduring relationships with religious communities in foreign settings, dialogue and respectful disagreement with people of faith in foreign publics, promoting religious freedom and interreligious dialogue, or thoughtfully evaluating religious phenomena that affect U.S. foreign policy.

Expand Knowledge Resources

This book has cited a number of studies that call for expanding the knowledge resources available to U.S. government personnel on the many intersections of religion and world affairs. One example is the U.S.-Muslim Engagement Project's *Changing Course*, which argues that the United States requires an investment in "education on Islam and Muslims" comparable to American spending on math and science in the wake of Sputnik. True, there are pockets of knowledge and expertise in the government, be it academic training or field-based experience, but these knowledge nodes tend to be aleatory and disconnected. It is imperative that America invests in, expands, and deepens the intellectual resources available to U.S. government officials on these issues.

A necessary first step called for by the Chicago Council on Global Affairs and others is for the White House to immediately task departments and agencies to provide a government-wide inventory of existing or recent efforts to build religious awareness as well as past experience and expertise on such issues. This will provide a baseline for shared information and synergies on training, professional development, program viability, resource needs, and opportunities for collaboration. White House "taskers," particularly those which issue from the National Security Council, generate rapid action in the Beltway and thus such an inventory should only take a few weeks to consolidate. Some government officials suggest that such an inventory has occurred, but it is not publicly available nor does it appear to be accessible to many in the foreign policy community. Likewise, the State Department recently did an internal survey of embassy and Department engagement with and on religious factors. Although this survey is not publicly available, it should be a welcome addition to the internal strategic awareness of the Department.

A second step in expanding intellectual resources is a commitment to integrating a basic level of religious literacy into the standardized training of diplomatic, military, aid, and intelligence officers. Regardless of agency, American foreign affairs professionals should have formal religious and cultural training at various points in their careers, including introductory training on religious dynamics in international affairs and follow-up training during the course of their careers.

Religious literacy implies basic training on the conceptual tools with which to approach the varied ways that religious factors may infuse political life. Religious literacy is a willingness to consider how identity—including those based in ideology, race, ethnicity, and nationalism—may be intertwined with religion and what that means for U.S. engagement and interests. Religiously aware diplomats are exposed to the nexus of religious themes and normative concerns such as human rights, the rights of women and minorities, race relations, and religion's potential for conflict or peace. In addition, religious literacy considers the many possibilities for U.S. government partnership with civil society and religious actors on critical issues such as political and economic development, security, poverty, disease, religious freedom, governance, and human rights. One recent, promising endeavor is the U.S. Air Force's creation of the Air Force Culture and Language Center, which not only provides incentives for airmen to learn foreign languages, but also provides professional military training with knowledge resources on culture and religion.

Third, in addition to a baseline level of knowledge, the U.S. government should cultivate a professional cadre of religious affairs specialists with deep expertise on religious and cultural factors in international security and foreign contexts. One area where such expertise is developing is in a series of publications produced by the U.S. Institute of Peace (USIP) about instances where religious actors have been or are currently engaged in bringing security, peace, justice, and/or reconciliation to conflict and postconflict situations.[8] Several of USIP's publications explicitly note the challenges in this area of scholarship and practice, perhaps most importantly the difficulty of comprehensively measuring the success of faith-based peacebuilding (beyond mere anecdotes) as well as the impediments to inculcating this material into the formal training and practice of government foreign affairs experts.

A fourth opportunity is to learn from others. The U.S. government could expand its knowledge resources on engaging religious actors by studying the best practices of other Western governments, international institutions, and multilateral fora. For instance, the World Bank and the Archbishop of Canterbury launched the World Faiths Development Dialogue in 1998 to enhance dialogue and action on development policies worldwide, which has become an important venue for discussing government policies and the involvement of faith communities in fighting poverty. The United States could learn from the experiences of its friends and allies—foreign ministries, development agencies, militaries—on a much broader set of issues. Such issues include understanding specific religiously inspired political parties (e.g., Christian Democrats, Turkey's AKP), religious themes and actors in economic development, the promise and peril of religious narratives in health campaigns (e.g., AIDS/HIV, reproductive health, contraception), coalitions and divisions in global environmental politics, religious claims and counterclaims in democratization and institution building, intended and unintended linkages to U.S. international religious freedom policy, religious actors and arguments in the global economic crisis, and faith-based and secular justifications for (and contradictions between) human rights. In short, the global resurgence of religion makes it imperative that the United States improve its knowledge resources and expertise.

Improve Its Assets

The American government is a massive, powerful entity with many resources and assets at its disposal. It has stockpiles ready to meet the threat of a pandemic, trained professionals and elaborate protocols for diplomacy, the mightiest military arsenal in world history, and deep stores of scientific and financial capital invested in fighting poverty and expanding economic development. What it lacks, however, is long-term, systematic, and comprehensive investment in the assets necessary for successful foreign policy in an increasingly religious world. Some of those invaluable assets include human capital, partnerships, education, and the religious capital of the American public.

The previous section argued for integrating a baseline of religious literacy in the formal training of foreign affairs officials, regardless of agency, as well as cultivating a professional cadre of government religious affairs specialists with deeper expertise. Some national leaders recognize existing limitations in this area. For instance, in 2008 former Secretary Gates issued a clarion call for increased "Religious and Ideological Studies" to counter what he calls "one of the most significant intellectual challenges we face."[9] The services have responded with some modest investments, such as a one-person Center for World Religions housed at the U.S. Army Chaplains School and "culture centers of excellence" at U.S. Central Command and Air (Force) University.

Another potential area of military innovation is the chaplaincy. Traditionally, U.S. military chaplains had an internal mission: provide for the rights of their troops to worship freely, even in highly constrained or combat conditions ("religious support"). However, in individual cases chaplains have increasingly taken on an external role in building bridges with local faith communities. This ad hoc approach began in the Balkans, but has become much more robust in Afghanistan and especially Iraq—often at the request of local Muslim leaders or military commanders. There are numerous stories of Muslim sheikhs, when meeting with United States or Coalition commanders, expressing surprise that the commander's "holy man" is not in the room or, worse, demanding to know why there is no chair and placard for the local imam at the table. In some instances chaplains were able to de-escalate tensions.

> ... the Brigade had raided a Shia mosque two weeks prior and arrested 18 militants. This caused great concern among regional "local religious leaders" (LRLs). Representatives from the national level of Shia religious leaders were sent to Kirkuk... I [the chaplain] visited the detainees (18 militants) in the detention facility and brought our Islamic chaplain... and talked to them (detainees) for over an hour. This visitation and the meeting set the stage for an important meeting that occurred a week later. I was the first American invited inside this Shia mosque since the Coalition Forces arrived in March 2003... Following this meeting, they (Shia religious leaders) agreed to meet with the company commander of that sector and have now established a working relationship with the command. The imam was grateful that we visited the detainees who were members of his mosque. This was simply a pastoral visitation, but it was significant in the eyes of the members of that mosque... The breakthrough we achieved with the Shia Muslims was an agreement that they would engage with the company commander, open lines of communication with Coalition Forces, prohibit weapons in the mosque, temper their violent anti-coalition language, submit to monitoring of their Friday messages, and begin working towards a mosque renovation project... This engagement indirectly saved lives—the lives of our soldiers.[10]

Chaplains are increasingly called upon to serve as religious advisors to combatant commanders, intermediaries ("religious leader liaisons") with local communities, observers at peace talks, and communication channels with tribal and religious leaders. This evolution of their duties is not without controversy, most vociferously within the chaplain corps itself. However, in November 2009 the Defense Department published Joint Publication 1-05, "Religious Affairs in Joint Operations." For the first time, military doctrine expanded the role of chaplains beyond religious support to officially include, at the direction of the commander and within the scope of their role as noncombatants, "religious leader engagement" (outreach to local religious leaders) and "religious advisement" (providing commanders with a sense of the religious sentiments of the area and the possible religious and cultural consequences of action).[11]

A next step for government agencies would be the development of a religion subspecialty, under existing career tracks, in the Foreign Service as well as in other major U.S. governmental organizations with an international focus (e.g., Defense, USAID). Religion specialists, as Albright asserts, should be seated at every country desk (in Washington, D.C.) where religion plays a major role in society, regardless of department or agency. Likewise, in countries characterized by highly religious publics, U.S. embassies and missions should have a religious affairs officer or "religious attaché" whose primary portfolio involves understanding and engaging religious communities and issues.[12] Developing such a corps within the larger foreign policy establishment would be a tremendous asset for the United States.

Another critical asset for U.S. foreign policy is relationships. More specifically, the U.S. government should seek out and build respectful relationships with major social and political actors in foreign settings, both in and out of government, including religious and faith-based leaders, communities, organizations, political parties, and interfaith fora. "Major actors" include those leaders of communities who are legitimate to their constituencies, whether through political legitimacy conferred by ballot or alternative notions of legitimacy based on position, experience, relationships, hereditary title, scholarship, or action. A better way to think about how religiously literate diplomacy builds relationships is a broader engagement strategy that takes into account the real centers of power and authority within a society and/or those who are the most effective service providers within the rule of law, not simply the elites and their cronies in the capital.

For instance, the United States has a long track record of partnership in working with private and faith-based organizations in the areas of humanitarian assistance and economic development. For example, a World Health Organization study of 11 African countries found that faith-based organizations provided up to half of all health services in those countries; many of these programs rely heavily on a mixture of denominational remittances and support from the United States and other Western governments.[13]

A final set of vital assets are already at the doorstep of Washington: its populace and nongovernmental institutions. The U.S. government should call upon the rich religious capital of the American citizenry, civil society, and higher education to provide resources for religious knowledge, interreligious dialogue, and expertise on specific religions and cultures. This capital is vital to U.S. foreign policy when engaging a religious world, and should provide the United States with a comparative advantage over its secular Western European counterparts when interacting with religious societies in Latin America, Asia, Africa, Eastern Europe, and the greater Middle East.

The American public is a highly religious society when compared with other Western countries. It has a unique history and present characterized by evolving religious freedom, pluralism, robust competition, and debate over belief and the proper role of faith in society. Its history of immigration and the numerous religious diaspora communities present make it a uniquely diverse religious landscape, and one in which representatives of all the world's major religions—as well as those who do not choose to believe or participate—live in relative harmony. These people and their experiences are a tremendous asset and as such, the government should consult American Muslims, Hindus, Christians, Jews, Buddhists, and others on such issues as appropriate.

Similarly, American higher education is the best in the world, and has developed significant resources for understanding religion and world affairs despite universities' typically secularist bent. American universities and think tanks need to respond to the reality of the global resurgence of religion by investing in teaching, programming, research, and exchange on the diverse nexus of religion and society.

Establish a Political Strategy

This book has argued that the United States needs to develop religiously literate foreign policy in order to comprehend and succeed in the current global landscape. This chapter has advocated for clear objectives and legal guidance from senior leadership, considerable investment in new knowledge resources, and the development or acquisition of new assets for the government's foreign policy apparatus. These actions should inform and intertwine a broader political strategy for engaging religious dynamics in world affairs, from presidential action to public diplomacy.

It is beyond the scope of this book to elucidate a comprehensive strategy that operationalizes the complete universe of objectives and tactics on religion and foreign policy appropriate to all federal agencies with any degree of sophistication. Nonetheless, it can point to some important elements of such a strategy beyond those in the first three recommendations. One component of a strategy to engage a world of resurging religion is for the president or secretary of state to formally address the topic, speaking candidly about the challenges and opportunities of American diplomacy maturing in this area. Such a speech would not only signal America's respect and interest in the values of foreign societies to the world, but would provide an aperture for new thinking and entrepreneurial action—with political cover—by U.S. foreign affairs experts. As noted earlier in this chapter, remarks by Obama in his inaugural address, at the 2009 National Prayer Breakfast, and especially in his Cairo speech, attempted to do this. However, at present the president seems to be a "voice crying in the wilderness"; no similar language has been heard from other senior administration officials nor is it clear that concrete action has been taken to implement the aspirations of the "the New Beginning."

A key component of a global political strategy is public diplomacy. The United States needs public diplomacy leaders who understand and can communicate the religious dimension of international affairs and foreign diplomacy—including the legal, ethical, and religious—elements of American commitments to democracy, religious freedom, and human rights. Public diplomacy is what (and how) American identity, values, and activities are communicated to foreign publics. In order to do public diplomacy well, it is important that religious actors and communities be targeted for engagement and that U.S. government messages be culturally relevant to foreign publics. This includes appreciating the deep values and sentiments of other nations, particularly those whose identities and social structures are infused with religion. However, this approach will fail if U.S. public diplomacy pretends religion does not exist. The U.S. National Strategy for Public Diplomacy and Strategic Communications (2007) cautioned, "if possible, avoid using religious language, because it can mean different things and is easily misconstrued." A better position would include caution at giving offense informed by thoughtful training on appropriate religious and cultural sentiments and mores.

Public diplomacy also requires listening and understanding the perspectives and priorities of other societies. One critical issue for public diplomacy rooted in religious dynamics is recent survey data which indicate that in some parts of the Muslim world, as much as 80 percent of the populace believes that the United States is at war with Islam or intends to "weaken and divide the Islamic world."[14] Recognizing, acknowledging, and overcoming this perception must be a foreign policy imperative for the United States.

It can start with robust public diplomacy, particularly with regard to two facts. The first, as argued by Imam Feisal Abdul Rauf, Ambassador Akbar Ahmed, and others is that Muslims enjoy greater freedom to live and worship in the United States than anywhere in the world.[15] The second is that the United States has been a good friend to Muslims in other countries, but has done a poor job of burnishing its record. It was the United States that led the international campaign that saved mostly Muslim Kosovo in 1999 and supported it in the years that followed just as it was America that finally goaded the Europeans into action that led to the Dayton Accords (and saved countless Bosnian Muslims) in 1995. Kosovo is part of a pattern of American leadership on issues that support the human and political rights of the Muslim everyman, from Europe to Sudan to the Far East. It is the United States that heavily supported the Afghans in their fight against the Soviets, and likewise liberated Afghanistan from the cruel Taliban and its al Qaeda associates. It is the United States that liberated 25 million Iraqis from the tyrannical Hussein regime, despite U.S. errors in securing the peace. It was the United States, and United States alone, that called the gross human rights violations against Muslims and non-Muslims in Darfur "genocide" and urged the Security Council to act. It was the United States that opened Libya and dismantled its nuclear program, reached out to Muslim populations in places like Indonesia and Malaysia, and it is the United States, somewhat uniquely in the West, which has made a practice of tough behind-the-scenes dialogue on tolerance, democracy, and human rights in places like Cairo while criticizing European capitals for restricting minaret construction and head scarves. However, one would not know this from our public diplomacy efforts.

In addition, the United States believes that the world is a marketplace of ideas and that some American normative commitments are worthy of advocacy, argument, and investment. This is another aspect of public diplomacy: robustly asserting and explaining American values such as human rights, democracy, and international religious freedom. The United States has seen numerous small successes, persuading regimes to release individual democracy activists, journalists, and religious imprisoned or persecuted for their view.[16] This is a form of public diplomacy that advances the debate on universal human rights and can positively impact individual human beings. The same is true for public diplomacy efforts on behalf of democracy to support and nourish representative institutions and civil liberties around the globe. Former President Clinton recognized that religion and democracy need not be antithetical. "At their best, religion and democracy respect the equality and value of every human being: all are stamped with the Creator's image, each endowed with certain inalienable rights," said Clinton. "These doctrines sit next to one another comfortably; they are unifying and inclusive."[17]

The U.S. government has recently turned far greater attention to foreign civil societies, rather than just government elites, as a place to nurture localized, representative governance and the habits of tolerance, pluralism, and political fair play. In highly religious societies the most important civil society actors may be denominational structures, houses of worship, or other faith-based organizations. The U.S. government may differ on many issues with such associations, but in practice the vitality of civil society requires a breadth of views and the freedom to express them. American support for programming in support of civil society and raising awareness on how civil society undergirds democracy can advance democracy worldwide. USAID and the State Department have been involved in some such efforts, providing funds to civil society groups—including Christian and Muslim councils—that formed an "Electoral Observatory" to impartially monitor Mozambique's municipal elections in 2003 and convening religious and civil society leaders on environmental issues in the Philippines that created a religiously and culturally informed environmental law.[18]

The United States will continue to advance sustainable democracy in its public diplomacy efforts because the spread of human liberty, free societies, representative government, and the rule of law is commensurate with America's deepest values and national interests. Religious themes, from freedom of religion to culturally relevant justifications for human rights, are a necessary component of public diplomacy in some settings for advancing democracy. Such efforts, in and of themselves, are not cultural imperialism or overbearing if handled with respect and sensitivity. Indeed, nearly every government is a signatory to the major international covenants promoting human rights, representative government, and religious liberty, so American messaging should be seen as exhorting, not excoriating.

Conclusion

This chapter has argued for a whole-of-government approach to understanding and engaging the multidimensionality of religion in world affairs. That approach should begin with senior leaders rethinking outdated practices and assumptions of the Old Diplomacy and "transforming" to the New Diplomacy. Senior leaders must articulate the importance of these issues and empower the foreign policy and national security establishments to integrate religious literacy and expertise into the training, planning, and execution of foreign policy. The approach includes expanding the array of assets available to the men and women who craft foreign policy on a day-to-day basis, to include knowledge resources, religious affairs specialists and liaisons at embassies and military bases as well as building relationships and partnerships with religious actors and organizations. The chapter also calls for a political strategy that ranges from presidential engagement to a major investment in holistic public diplomacy.

However critical questions remain: Does this matter for the day-to-day business of U.S. national security and foreign policy in 2009 and beyond?

Would the implementation of these recommendations mean a different set of U.S. foreign policies? A better set of policies? The next two chapters will address these questions, particularly with respect to international religious freedom, human rights, democracy promotion, and faith's intersection with war and peace.

CHAPTER 7

Liberty, Democracy, and Development

In February 2006 Abdul Rahman was arrested in his native Afghanistan. Rahman had converted to Christianity 16 years earlier while working for a Christian NGO in Peshawar, Pakistan. He left the region and worked in Germany for 9 years, returning in 2002. Rahman says that he returned in order to gain custody of his daughters, who had been living with his parents. His parents contacted authorities that their son had converted to Christianity; a Bible was found in his possession.

The judge trying the case issued the following statement:

> The Attorney General is emphasizing he should be hung. It is a crime to convert to Christianity from Islam. He is teasing and insulting his family by converting...we are not against any particular religion in the world. But in Afghanistan, this sort of thing is against the law. It is an attack on Islam.[1]

Other influential Afghan clerics urged the use of the death penalty as well. The chief cleric at Haji Yacob Mosque said,

> The government is scared of the international community. But the people will kill him if he is freed...There will be an uprising. The government will lose the support of the people. What sort of democracy would it be if the government ignored the will of all the people?

A member of the Afghan Ulama Council demanded, "The government is playing games. The people will not be fooled. Cut off his head! We will call on the people to pull him into pieces so there's nothing left." Mirhossain Nasri of the Hossainia Mosque asserted,

> We must set an example...He must be hanged...We are a small country and we welcome the help the outside world is giving us, but please don't interfere in this issue. We are Muslims and these are our beliefs. This is much more important to us than all the aid the world has given us.[2]

Clearly Rahman and his family had stirred up a hornet's nest, demonstrating not only the salience of communal identity and religious faith, but inconsistencies in Afghan jurisprudence and the significant social standing of clerics.

In late March 2006, Rahman was freed. It is clear that tremendous international pressure was brought on President Hamid Karzai; the court apparently dismissed the case due to "lack of evidence." Because Rahman remained in mortal danger, he was spirited out of the country.

Is it possible that the United States and its freedom-loving European allies rescued the Afghan people from the Taliban, decimated the ranks of al Qaeda, and invested billions of dollars in the people and infrastructure of Afghanistan only to establish a repressive, authoritarian regime? Indeed, how is it possible that the United States tutored the Afghan parliament through nearly a decade of investment and the writing of its constitution—one that guarantees individual freedoms and reasserts Afghanistan's international commitments under the International Covenant on Civil and Political Rights (including religious freedom)—only to find that Afghanistan again is ranked "not free" by Freedom House and is characterized as one of the world's most egregious violators of religious liberty and human rights by the State Department?

The Afghan case reminds America of the perils and promise of considering religious factors in U.S. foreign policy. One simply cannot understand Afghanistan without some appreciation of religious and cultural characteristics. Hence the U.S. foreign policy establishment needs to have some measure of religious literacy when engaging Afghanistan and clearly think through the ramifications of American values commitments to religious rights of Christians and minority Shia (Hazara) in Afghanistan, secular "family planning" programs in highly religious Uganda, or funding "Islam and Civil Society" programming in Indonesia. This chapter looks at the intersection of religion's many dimensions with key U.S. foreign policy imperatives in the areas of economic development, sustainable democracy promotion, and human rights and religious freedom. Religious literacy is only the beginning; an effective U.S. foreign policy will advance the value of individual liberty and human rights on the global stage while strategically partnering in many instances with the ubiquitous, trusted networks of religious people on the ground.

Human Rights Policy and Religion

Human rights—the concept that all human beings have certain intrinsic rights because they are human—are rooted in the American political tradition and in the evolutionary struggles of American society over two centuries. The founding narrative of U.S. history is that among the earliest pioneers to the New World were those seeking religious and other forms of liberty, understood as their essential rights. The same holds true today, as religious minorities and hundreds of thousands of others every year seek a better life in the United States, where political liberty, property rights, a free press, freedom of association and assembly, judicial due process, and other rights are considered by Americans as fundamental, natural, and constitutive of representative government. Moreover, American history is replete with rights champions, from Patrick Henry and those who fought the Revolutionary War to abolitionists like William Lloyd Garrison, to humanitarian "angels" like Florence Nightingale, to Eleanor Roosevelt's impassioned work on behalf of the United Nations, to civil rights leaders like Martin Luther King, Jr.

Nonetheless, from the time of America's founding onward, the notion of rights and religion is an imperfect association in at least two ways. The first is that not all religious voices champion a universal notion of rights. Faith-groups, just like any other human collective, can be politically exclusivist, providing religious and other forms of justification for hierarchies of rights and erecting barriers to equality. Often, the most passionate critics of religio-political exclusivism are people of faith.

A second observation is that since the atrocities of World War II, an alternative, secular track in human rights thinking developed, even if it has religious allies. Major portions of the contemporary human rights movement, launched following the Holocaust, have a secular, globalist bent that defines human rights broadly. One of the motivations of secular human rights advocacy is rooted in an old critique of the religious basis for rights. Two centuries ago British philosopher Jeremy Bentham criticized religious (natural law) definitions of individual rights: "Right is a child of law; from real laws come real rights, but from imaginary law, from 'laws of nature,' come imaginary rights...Natural rights is simple nonsense."[3] However, religious actors strenuously rebut Bentham's positivism, countering that laws come and go, but it is a universalist notion of rights rooted in a religious conception of humanity's dignity as children of God that best advances human rights for all.

Thus, U.S. history is a complex story of advances, and sometimes setbacks, in the realization of rights. Religious communities and religious understandings were key players in many of the great rights movements, from the debate over the Bill of Rights to abolition, from Progressive-era reforms to women's suffrage and civil rights. Religious people joined others in pushing the United States to write or sign the Universal Declaration of Human Rights, the International Covenant on Political and Civil Rights and international covenants against Slavery, Genocide, and Torture. And in the past decade, religious Americans led a string of human rights victories: the International Religious Freedom Act (1998), the Trafficking in Persons Act (2000), the Sudan Peace Act (2002), and the North Korea Human Rights Act (2004).[4] However, the sad fact remains that many religious actors were on the wrong side of these issues over the course of U.S. history, most notably many Southern churches on the issues of slavery and race. Today America recognizes the dialectical nature of the historical process establishing rights for all citizens in the United States as well as the political reality that a web of statutes and court decisions helped make general principles a lived reality.

There can be a reluctance to engage religious actors abroad on any variety of policy programs and issues due to a concern that they are regressive when it comes to rights. In other words, the conservative and often patriarchal nature of religious establishments has at times set them at odds with the human rights activists and/or U.S. foreign policy. However, ignoring their existence is simply not an option; religious actors are centers of gravity in human rights debates.

President Ronald Reagan's ambassador to South Africa recognized this. Reagan had charged Ambassador Edward Perkins, who previously engaged Liberian dictator Samuel Doe, with helping to dismantle apartheid. Perkins, America's first black ambassador to South Africa, decided to approach South African society along numerous fronts, including public and private interaction with key religious actors. Early in his tenure, Perkins deliberately attended prominent all-white churches as well as black and mixed congregations, making national headlines. He met privately with nationally known pastors and the heads of segregated religious denominations, including the pro-apartheid Dutch Reformed Church. Perkins was often challenged about the state of American race relations and he could point to his own experience as a native Louisianan as well as the triumphs of the civil rights movement—led by pastors and people of faith—in officially ending segregation and establishing the Civil Rights Act. The U.S. government was thus a critical voice in urging South Africa toward ending apartheid, and it did so by engaging multiple sectors of politics and society.[5]

What does all of this mean for U.S. foreign policy? First, the U.S. historical experience should make Americans thankful for the monumental achievements of their forbears and thoughtful about how difficult and intractable such change can prove. Second, the global task is far from complete: the past decade has been a turbulent era with human rights advances in some regions and an erosion of human rights in others. Human trafficking, religious persecution, torture, extrajudicial punishment, and ethnic cleansing continue. Furthermore, the formal human rights organs of the United Nations continue to come under scrutiny for seating gross human rights violators. Third, while the United States was long considered the foremost leader in advancing human rights, recent events such as the Abu Ghraib scandal have caused concerns about this commitment. Secretary of State Hillary Rodham Clinton recently underscored the U.S. commitment to human rights: "A mutual and collective commitment to human rights is [as] important to bettering our world as our efforts on security, global economics, energy, climate change, and other pressing issues."[6] However, the world seems to be cautiously evaluating whether the United States' words are consistent with its stated values.

Despite its flaws and limitations, the United States must continue to provide moral and practical leadership on these issues. The U.S. government must continue to explicitly support human rights worldwide, and it should do so contextually, communicating the value of such rights in culturally and religiously relevant language in the societies that are being engaged. President Obama said as much in 2009: "What those of us of religious faith have to do when we're in the public square is to translate our language into a universal language that can appeal to everybody."[7] Important arenas where the United States is particularly well-suited to lead are international religious freedom and supporting democracy.

International Religious Freedom Policy

Religious freedom is a fundamental right, inextricably linked to a variety of other notions of freedom: worship, conscience, speech, press, assembly, and the like. Religious freedom is part of America's founding narrative and the United States continues to be a consistent champion of religious liberty both home and abroad. From the perspective of most U.S. citizens, it is simply impossible to conceive of a situation where basic human rights were observed without religious freedom or a situation where true religious freedom—including the right to change or leave religion—exists where other human rights are in jeopardy.

The United States is not alone. A recent Pew Global Attitudes survey (cited above) found that over 90 percent of the people in the 46 countries surveyed say that religious freedom is important to them. Religious freedom is associated with the fundamental liberty of the individual to believe in and make choices about matters of faith. American citizens tend to see religious freedom as an inherent right, one that is expressly enumerated and protected in the First Amendment of the Constitution:

"Congress shall make no law respecting an establishment of religion, or prohibiting the free exercise thereof; or abridging the freedom of speech, or of the press; or the right of the people peaceably to assemble, and to petition the Government for a redress of grievances."

The United States also has a long tradition of supporting religious freedom within the modern human rights framework, most notably as a signatory of the Universal Declaration of Human Rights and the International Covenant of Civil and Political Rights.

Created in 1966, the International Covenant on Civil and Political Rights is a United Nations treaty that took on the force of law in 1976. This treaty is legally binding and has been signed by nearly every government in the world.

Article 18

1. Everyone shall have the right to freedom of thought, conscience and religion. This right shall include freedom to have or to adopt a religion or belief of his choice, and freedom, either individually or in community with others and in public or private, to manifest his religion or belief in worship, observance, practice and teaching.

2. No one shall be subject to coercion which would impair his freedom to have or to adopt a religion or belief of his choice.

3. Freedom to manifest one's religion or beliefs may be subject only to such limitations as are prescribed by law and are necessary to protect public safety, order, health, or morals or the fundamental rights and freedoms of others.

In addition to its multilateral commitments, the United States has undertaken concrete actions to promote religious liberty worldwide for nearly four decades. That leadership began in the U.S. Congress during the Cold War with concern for the plight of Soviet Jews and later Soviet Pentecostals. In 1974 Congress passed the Jackson-Vanik Amendment, which linked trade relations with the Soviet Union to the freedom of Jews and others to emigrate. The following year, the Helsinki Accords resolved the territorial status of the Soviet Union, linking that issue to a substantive human right agenda that included religious freedom.

Two decades later, an unusual coalition of human rights and religious liberty organizations presented Congress with evidence of religious persecution of Christians worldwide. Not all of those lobbying for Congressional action were Christians—Jews, Baha'is, and other faiths were represented as were secular human rights advocates.[8]

Ultimately, President Clinton signed the International Religious Freedom Act of 1998 (IRFA), which can be summarized as:

● Declared "The right to freedom of religion undergirds the very origin and existence of the United States...as a fundamental right and as a pillar of our Nation...Freedom of religious belief and practice is a universal human right and fundamental freedom…"

- Created an independent U.S. Commission on International Religious Freedom (USCIRF) to make recommendations to the president and Congress.
- Designated an Ambassador-at-Large for International Religious Freedom at the U.S. Department of State, leading an Office of International Religious Freedom.
- Mandated an Annual Report on International Religious Freedom to include every country in the world.
- Provided a menu of options for U.S. government action to name, shame, and punish violators of religious freedom, with a special focus on "Countries of Particular Concern."
- Called for institutionalized training, programming, and recognition for U.S. diplomats engaged in this work.

After IRFA's 10-year anniversary in 2008, numerous events and documents evaluated the Act's accomplishments, including a book by the first director of the State Department's Office of International Religious Freedom, Thomas Farr. A summary of these documents and proceedings suggests several areas where proponents say IRFA has succeeded.[9] The first is simply, but importantly, the institutionalization of religious freedom advocacy by the U.S. government in the Department of State as well as at the independent commission. Proponents of IRFA argue that these structures put "flesh on the bones" of international covenants like the UDHR and ICCPR, calling on other governments to live up to their promises. The State Department's annual report on international religious freedom is widely considered to be the "gold-standard" of such reporting worldwide and is referenced by some Western governments in formulating their own policies. At the individual level, there are several cases worldwide where individuals imprisoned or persecuted for their faith have benefited from the local intervention of a U.S. ambassador on their behalf. Although many of the most appalling violators, such as Myanmar (Burma) and Saudi Arabia, remain hostile to this understanding of religious liberty, there have been some modest successes. For instance, in 2006 the State Department removed Vietnam from the list of Countries of Particular Concern, which sets the country up for sanctions and makes Most Favored Nation trade status impossible, after it released a number of prisoners held on religious charges and ended a number of restrictions on churches and other houses of worship. Vietnam, however, demonstrates just how difficult progress can be on these issues. In January 2011 an American political officer was severely beaten when trying to visit a Catholic priest who is under house arrest. This egregious attack is emblematic of increased restrictions since 2007 on faith-based organizations and persecution of people of faith, particularly Christians.[10]

However, even IRFA's staunchest defenders recognize numerous weaknesses to be remedied. From a structural perspective, the State Department's religious freedom office is located on the bureaucratic periphery and the Ambassador-at-Large for International Religious Freedom reports to a lower-ranking Assistant Secretary of State rather than directly to the Secretary. This arrangement suggests a deeper philosophical problem in international religious freedom policy—that IRFA is poorly integrated into the broader range of diplomatic initiatives to support democracy and advance human rights abroad. Part of this may be due to reluctance within some elements of the diplomatic and security communities to make promotion of religious freedom a key activity of U.S. foreign engagement, perhaps because of a concern of offending foreign governments or secularist skepticism of the merit of such approaches. Indeed, most of the time and energy of the Office of International Religious Freedom and the Commission is spent on developing annual reports and identifying discrete cases of persecution, rather than a comprehensive effort to expand religious freedom.

Finally, there are additional reasons that other countries are skeptical of international religious freedom, notably a desire to maintain religious monopolies and/or protect culture from outside interference or proselytization. In some cases, such as Russia, an alliance has developed between the central government and "national" religious authorities (in this case the Russian Orthodox Church) to exclude "outside" religions. Elsewhere, the notions of citizenship are intimately tied to shared ethnoreligious identities, making religious freedom sound like a challenge to essential citizenship. Some argue that the United States focuses too much on the plight of Christians, although the State Department reports also advocate on behalf of Muslims, Jews, Hindus, Baha'is, and even Scientologists.

What is the state of international religious freedom today? In testimony before the Senate Foreign Affairs Committee, Pew Research Center scholar Brian Grimm reported,

> Our study finds that 64 nations, or about one-third of countries today, have high restrictions on religion either as a result of government restrictions or social hostilities involving religion, or both. Because some of the most restrictive countries are very populous, that means about 70 percent of the world's population lives in countries with high or very high restrictions on religion, the brunt of which often falls on religious minorities.

Grimm went on to say, "First, considering *government restrictions*":

- In two-thirds of countries, some level of government interfered with worship or other religious practices, including religious expression and affiliation.

- In nearly half of countries, members of one or more religious groups were killed, physically abused, imprisoned, detained or displaced from their homes by some state or local government actor.
- In more than a quarter of countries, there was widespread government intimidation of one or more religious groups.
- In nearly a quarter of countries, the national government did not intervene in cases of discrimination or abuses against religious groups.
- In more than 80 percent of countries, governments clearly discriminated against one or more religious groups by giving preferential support or favors to some religious group(s) and not others.
- In 60 percent of countries, registration requirements for religious groups adversely affected their ability to operate, or the requirements clearly discriminated against certain religious groups.

And next, considering *social hostilities involving religion:*

- In more than 70 percent of countries, there were crimes, malicious acts or violence motivated by religious hatred or bias.
- In more than 10 percent of countries, there were acts of sectarian or communal violence between religious groups.
- In nearly 90 percent of countries, public tensions between or within religious groups were present, and these tensions involved violence in more than six-in-ten countries.
- In 30 percent of countries, religion-related terrorist groups were active in recruitment or fundraising. Such groups committed violent acts in nearly one-in-ten countries.
- In more than half of countries, religious groups themselves attempted to prevent other religious groups from being able to operate.
- In nearly a third of countries, individuals were assaulted or displaced from their homes in retaliation for specific religious activities considered offensive or threatening to the majority faith, including preaching and other forms of religious expression.[11]

These statistics suggest that there is more work to be done on these issues in the early twenty-first century. The consideration of the United States' moral commitment to human rights in theory and the practical, day-to-day business of defending and promoting such rights—like religious freedom—turns the chapter's attention to a related set of policies consistent with central commitments of U.S. identity and policy: support for international democracy.

Religion and Sustainable Democracy

The notion of supporting democracy abroad has long been part of U.S. foreign policy, particularly since the end of World War II. As one Jennifer Windsor observed, "advancing freedom is an expression of the United States' most sacred ideals" and has an "established parentage" of American executives, including Presidents Franklin D. Roosevelt, Harry S. Truman, John F. Kennedy, Jimmy Carter, Ronald Reagan, and Bill Clinton.[12] Those "sacred ideals" were signed into law by the 110th Congress' Advance Democracy Act (2007), which states:

> It is the policy of the United States to promote freedom and democracy in foreign countries as a fundamental component of the United States foreign policy...to affirm fundamental freedoms and international recognized human rights...to condemn offenses against those freedoms and rights as a fundamental component of United States foreign policy...to protect and promote such fundamental freedoms and rights, including the freedoms of association, of expression, of the press, and of religion, and the right to own private property; to commit to the long-term challenge of promoting universal democracy...to support...free, fair, and open elections,...to strengthen cooperation with other democratic countries...

Democratization was a roller-coaster in the 1990s, with the promise and some disappointments in the Color Revolutions, the Arab Spring, and fledgling new governance structures in Kabul, Baghdad, Kosovo and the Palestinian Authority. President Bush called for a "freedom agenda" to advance democracy, and that will likely continue. Indeed, one political scientist argues that President Obama will "out-freedom" Bush.[13] In a major address to the Chicago Council on Global Affairs in 2007, then-candidate Obama said:

> We have heard much over the last six years about how America's larger purpose in the world is to promote the spread of freedom—that it is the yearning of all who live in the shadow of tyranny and despair...I agree. But this yearning is not satisfied by simply deposing a dictator and setting up a ballot box. The true desire of all mankind is not only to live free lives, but lives marked by dignity and opportunity; by security and simple justice...It also requires a society that is supported by the pillars of a sustainable democracy: a strong legislature, an independent judiciary, the rule of law, a vibrant civil society, a free press, and an honest police force. It requires building the capacity of the world's weakest states and providing them what they need to reduce poverty, build healthy and educated communities, develop markets, and generate wealth.[14]

Two years later, as president, Obama gave a speech in Cairo inaugurating a "New Beginning" between the American people and the Muslim world. President

Obama stunned many onlookers in the United States and abroad by addressing the fundamental human right of religious freedom. He observed, "Freedom in America is indivisible from freedom to practice one's religion," and later made religious freedom one of seven priority areas of challenge for the Muslim world. The president asserted, "People should be free to choose and live their faith based upon the persuasion of the mind and the heart and the soul." President Obama approvingly cited the ways that religious freedom is good for a society: respect for others, tolerance for diversity, interfaith dialogue, and "interfaith service...[such as] combating malaria in Africa, or providing relief after a natural disaster."[15] The speech went on in a simple yet elegant fashion to demonstrate the links between a series of bundled liberties: religious freedom, private property and economic growth, the need for (liberal arts and science) education, women's rights, and representative government.

With this in mind, what precisely is the nexus of religion and what President Obama called "sustainable democracy?" Better put, how can U.S. government efforts to secure and support democracy abroad engage religion appropriately and strategically?

Just as religious leaders and communities have played key roles in the expansion of democracy in the United States—most notably during the civil rights movement—the same is true in many other societies. Engaging such natural allies is nothing new; the United States partnered with Christian Democratic parties in Europe in the 1950s and 1960s and affirmed the global anti-Communism leadership roles of Pope John Paul II, some Latin American bishops, and various Muslim voices in the 1980s. The United States saw it in its interest to not exclude religious actors from the debate because many democracy activists are inspired by deep religious faith that motivates them to champion human rights, limits on excessive government power, and freedoms of religion and expression. Former President Clinton recognized this, saying,

> At their best, religion and democracy respect the equality and value of every human being: all are stamped with the Creator's image, each endowed with certain inalienable rights. These doctrines sit next to one another comfortably; they are unifying and inclusive.[16]

The U.S. government has recently turned far greater attention to foreign civil societies to nurture localized, representative governance and the habits of tolerance, pluralism, and political fair play. In highly religious societies the most important civil society actors may be denominational structures, houses of worship, or other faith-based organizations. The U.S. government may differ on many issues with such associations, but in practice the vitality of civil society requires a breadth of views and the freedom with which to express them.

Chapter 6 called for religious literacy in U.S. diplomacy characterized, in part, by the U.S. government engaging the major, legitimate social actors in a given country—including religious leaders. Such actors are buttresses of civil society, shapers of public opinion, and key players in the fluid world of national ideas. In fact, when dealing with highly religious societies, the United States should recognize them as potential strategic partners with far more credibility and reach than the average Western-oriented NGO. However, it is not only important to target the right social actors to nurture democracy; the message must ring true as well. Unfortunately, many people in highly religious societies—especially in the Muslim world—misunderstand the notions of "separation of church and state" in the American context to mean complete banishment of religion from the public sphere. Such radical privatization, combined with problematic notions of the "sovereignty of the people" as contrasted with the sovereignty of God, raises questions and barriers to some in the Muslim world.

Hence, some humility and optimism in recognizing the intersection of democracy, religion, and culture is necessary. Former Secretary of State Condoleezza Rice argued,

> Democracy is really the complex interplay of democratic practices and culture. In the experience of countless nations, ours especially, we see that culture is not destiny. Nations of every culture, race, religion, and level of development have embraced democracy and adapted it to their own circumstances and traditions.[17]

The United States needs to articulate to foreign publics how the U.S. citizenry can be robustly religious and how religion can influence public affairs without the U.S. government granting favoritism to any faith community. This approach is applicable to many religious societies. The American experience is not the sole model for emulation, nor should the U.S. demand a cookie-cutter approach, but it is descriptive of how a large nation has embraced religious freedom and pluralism, and how this strengthens constitutional government.

In fact, such an approach calls for a reordering of the elements of U.S. democracy promotion messages and activities away from simply focusing on institutions and toward advocating for a concept of bundled liberties. Too often Americans have placed our bets on, and been disappointed by, the procedures of voting or individual personalities, disregarding whether the society at large is actually characterized by the values system necessary for human liberty and representative government, including freedoms of speech, press, association, and religion.

Interestingly, research suggests a strong correlation between authoritarian governance and terrorism. One study suggests that 70 percent of terrorists originate under authoritarian systems. However, the research also suggests that religious actors, like India's Hindu-nationalist political party BJP or conservative Islamist parties elsewhere, can be inducted into the political process as has happened in Bangladesh, Indonesia, Malaysia, and Turkey. The United States has a mixed record on pushing authoritarian regimes to open to real competition. Thus, to support sustainable democracies America should consider each case contextually, with the assumption that those who are willing to play by the rules of the system, including religious parties, are partners.

President Obama argued for "sustainable democracy" that includes social, political, and economic forms of development. Socioeconomic development is discussed later in this chapter, but it is important to note at this point that not only do economic development and stable democracy go hand-in-hand, but religious freedom and pluralism appear to play a positive, contributing role as well. Indeed, this where religious freedom and human rights are inextricably bundled with the wider set of democratic liberties and mechanisms: one cannot have sustainable democracy without these freedoms. The scholarly evidence is fresh, timely, and compelling. For instance, one study of over 100 countries found that the presence of religious liberty directly correlates to other key democratic factors, including civil liberties, freedom of the press, the longevity of democracy, and an open economic environment.[18] Other studies have considered the "social capital" and the "spiritual capital" that result from involvement in religious and civic associations.[19] Religious groups increasingly bring their members tangible benefits and skills including literacy, vocational training, financial assistance in times of crisis,[20] experience managing people and finances; all of which can result not only in material benefits, but deeper and wider patterns of civic participation.[21]

Religious actors can be a part of the solution or the problem when it comes to political competition and conflict by promoting (or acquiescing to) government restrictions on religious freedom. A recent study published in the *American Sociological Review* found that social restrictions (social religious intolerance) lead to political restrictions on religious liberties, making sectarian violence more likely. In other words, when political authorities clamp down on religious practice and competition at the behest of religious social actors, tension and often violence is the result. Such is often the case in majority-religion countries with only small religious minorities. In contrast, countries that allow for religious freedom and competition develop what the study's authors call a "religious freedom cycle" that has positive benefits for society, from tolerance to wider civil liberties to deeper security in a stable political system.

In conclusion, the United States should not back down from sustainable democracy promotion because the spread of human liberty, free societies, representative government, and the rule of law is commensurate with America's deepest values and national interest. Religious themes, from freedom of religion to culturally relevant justifications for human rights, are a necessary component for advancing U.S. support for democracy in some settings. Religious institutions, from political parties to literacy groups to faith-based development and service organizations, have a role to play in meeting the needs of the weak and buttressing civil society. Religious leaders can be critical voices for fairness, the rule of law, tolerance, and representative governance. Championing such values, when handled with respect and sensitivity, is not overbearing or cultural imperialism. Indeed nearly every government is a signatory to the major international covenants promoting human rights, representative government, and religious liberty. Publics around the world look to the United States for leadership on these issues and such leadership is a critical part of American identity and commitment to the international community.

Religion, Socioeconomic Development, and U.S. Foreign Policy

International development is a central U.S. priority. Crisis assistance, humanitarian aid, and longer-term development support are integral parts of U.S. foreign policy and intersect frequently with faith agendas. Supporting international development has been a stated priority of recent presidential administrations, regardless of party, because the issue of equity is congruent with American values and vital for long-term global stability and human well-being. Indeed, a widespread consensus has developed that global health; socioeconomic progress, agriculture and trade; and democracy, conflict prevention and humanitarian assistance are at the heart of American ideals and interests in the developing world. It is not surprising, then, that these three areas are explicit dimensions of the mission of USAID and other U.S. international assistance programs. In addition, America continues to be a critical donor and partner to many global development initiatives such as the Millennium Development Goals.

Economic development specifically refers to generating sustainable economic success, but the concept implies a systemic approach by which a nation improves the economic, political, and social well-being of its people.[22] There is an obvious nexus of religious factors and development because many of the advocates for and practitioners of development services are motivated by religious impulses, operate faith-based organizations, or understand their work as a "calling." General themes of charity, caring for one's neighbor, and responsibility to help others are part of the larger American culture that supports economic development activities, be they by religious organizations, nonreligious groups, the federal government, or multilateral institutions. These general values find their spiritual counterparts in specific religious traditions, including tithing and charity in Islam, care for the stranger and the Jubilee in Judaism, the Golden Rule and the parable of the Good Samaritan in Christianity, and active notions of compassion in Buddhism and Hinduism.

Economic development as a key ingredient of U.S. foreign policy is largely a product of the postwar and postcolonial environment of the past half-century. During that time, some U.S. representatives developed expertise on the ground in engaging with religious actors, both those based in the United States (e.g., World Vision, Catholic Relief Services, American Jewish World Service) as well as the myriad of local associations, churches, mosques, and faith-based organizations in host countries.

The United States continues to rank as a leader in global development assistance, although the delivery of that service has evolved over time. In contrast to many other donor societies, the American tradition is one where a massive amount of overseas development funds flow through private secular and religious organizations rather than through the government. A definitive study by Harvard scholars of 1,639 U.S.-based religious and secular "private and voluntary organizations" (PVOs) involved in humanitarian assistance from 1939 to 2004 found that:

- An estimated 41 percent of U.S. overseas development funds are channeled through PVOs, in contrast to Japan (2 percent) and the United Kingdom (12 percent).
- Over six decades, the general breakdown of total American development revenues is 16.7 percent federal, 3.8 percent international organizations or other governments, and 79.5 percent private.
- From the mid-1980s to mid-1990s, secular groups led in funding; but by 2004 that funding was about even between secular and religious groups. Interestingly, because there are roughly twice as many secular PVOs, the average religious PVOs revenue are approximately double that of secular PVOs. Evangelical groups have seen the most growth over the past two decades, with some decline in Jewish groups.[23]

The Boston Globe tracked the specific allocations of such funds to faith-based organizations from fiscal year 2001 through fiscal year 2005. That study found that the percentage of USAID funding going to such groups rose from about 10 percent to 19 percent of USAID funding during that time period. In other words, 80–90 percent of USAID funding did not go to faith-based organizations. More specifically, 159 faith-based organizations received more than $1.7 billion in USAID contracts and grants during that time.[24]

With this background mind, there are at least five areas where faith meets development that require greater attention and sophistication from the U.S. government. The first should be glaringly obvious: the development activities of the U.S. government and its major partners are harmed when it is blind to, disregard, or antagonize faith-based economic development actors. It is entirely possible for development experts to miss both the religious themes and controversies attendant in some development issues as well as how religious actors can play key roles as experts, intermediaries, and service providers in host nations. Former USAID Administrator Andrew Natsios writes, "We must play to the strengths of multiple partners within recipient countries. Not all, by any stretch, are found in government. Many are found in civil society, in religious institutions..."[25] A forthcoming book on religion and international affairs includes an illustrative example. A survey team of social scientists prepared a social assessment in advance of an ambitious malaria-program in southern Africa. This was a sophisticated study conducted by thoughtful researchers who strategically engaged local and elected leaders as well as traditional authorities across that country, and its findings were nuanced and thoughtful. However, the study entirely failed to consult religious leaders on the topic because they were not considered in the development professionals' definition of "civil society."

This anecdote, from a possible legion, is a reminder that there are development circles in which religious factors are missed entirely as aid workers focus on secular groups and government structures. Churches, mosques, and other religious centers of gravity should be among the many focal points for U.S. efforts to improve the well-being of others through economic development. As two World Bank experts observe,

> Secular development practitioners today cannot do their jobs well without a basic understanding of the perspectives and work of faith organizations...This understanding will enhance the quality of program and also enable them to avoid pitfalls now too often obscured by lack of knowledge and active misunderstanding.[26]

However, being blind to or disregarding religious actors is not the only problem: it is entirely possible for U.S. development efforts to antagonize religious actors in ways detrimental to development goals and our relationships abroad. Consequently, enhancing religious literacy, as recommended in the previous chapter, is critical for refining the expertise of U.S. aid workers who work in developing countries with highly religious populations.

Second, the U.S. government needs to publicly recognize that global development is a multilateral enterprise. Whereas the power and resources of U.S. hard power dwarf the capabilities of the rest of the world—sometimes causing anxiety and resentment abroad—the development arena is far less contested and abounds with natural allies and tremendous opportunity for goodwill. Unlike strategic-military concerns where the United States continually wonders if its closest allies will make the hard commitments of money and manpower to participate as equals in international security, those allies heavily contribute to foreign aid to the developing world. Simply put, the massive scale of both short- and long-term need is such that cooperation is not only possible, it is vital.

The entire landscape of foreign assistance has evolved in at least two ways, the first being that the United States is no longer the largest per capita donor. Although America remains the largest real contributor as well as a critical leader in various multilateral organizations, others such as Norway, the Netherlands, Sweden, Luxembourg, and Denmark give a greater percentage of their GDP to foreign aid. The second change is that the public sector no longer dominates. As Natsios recounts:

In the 1970s, the US Federal Government was the largest source of funds flowing to the developing world. As a result, USAID normally defined a development problem and its solution internally, implementing activities through grants and contracts. Today, about 86 percent of resources are "private," meaning foreign direct investment, international bank loans and security investments, money sent home to countries by immigrants (what we call remittances), donations from corporations and corporate foundations, scholarships from universities and colleges, donations from faith-based groups, and finally donations from family foundations in the US.[27]

The United States rightfully has key concerns about the accountability of some multilateral bodies, such as the scandalous state of the UN oil-for-food program in Iraq during the 1990s. That being said, the international arena is a much broader avenue for cooperative engagement on development issues with other governments, through the Organization for Economic Co-operation and Development (OECD), various UN programs, nonstate actors, and transnational religious organizations committed to development. It is well-documented how such multilateral partnerships—coalitions of secular, government and religious bodies—are reframing the global development agenda on issues of debt (Jubilee 2000), poverty (the World Faiths Development Dialogue with the World Bank), and others.

The reasons that the United States needs to publicly recognize the multilateral nature of economic development are multifold. First, economic development is an area of principle and priority for the United States but global development is far beyond American resources—this is a huge task that necessitates major international collaboration to improve. The U.S. government should also recognize that religious actors are keenly aware of and often involved in major development initiatives worldwide, from working toward the Millennium Development Goals to poverty eradication, nutrition, clean water, health and sanitation, and the environment.

Third, the U.S. government needs to change its ambivalence toward bilateral engagement with religiously inspired development practitioners. USAID is a much smaller agency than it was a generation ago and U.S. development activities have proliferated, and diluted, across agencies to include the Departments of State, Defense, and Agriculture as well as specialized entities like the Millennium Challenge Corporation and the President's Emergency Plan for AIDS Relief (PEPFAR). The meta-trends in U.S. foreign assistance, such as the scaling down of USAID and the like, are beyond the scale of this report.

However, it is in the interest of the U.S. government to engage religious actors in U.S. economic development activities. U.S. government practitioners in the field have a long track record of partnering with religious actors in economic development. Religious actors are widely distributed across countries, have deep roots with or as members of the community, know the ground better than any outsider ever will, speak in culturally relevant communications, and tend to be trusted networks for support and assistance. A quick study demonstrates that in some of the world's poorest places, religious groups provide far more assistance—with or without help from foreign governments—to local citizens than do secular or governmental groups. It is often religious orders who not only provide the equivalent of the soup kitchen, but also are the primary and/or the best providers of education, healthcare, maternity services, training, and agricultural expertise.

This was demonstrated during a conference at Rick Warren's "purpose driven" Saddleback Church which focused on fighting HIV/AIDS in Africa. As one author tells it:

> A map of part of Rwanda...was projected high above the church (which holds 3,000 people)...first showed the three hospitals in the region, two of them

administered by religious groups. The region's 18 clinics—16 of them administered by faith groups—were then superimposed on the map. Finally, the hundreds of local churches were added, at which point it was nearly impossible to see any map details because the church dots obliterated them. The message was that no other network can rival the motivation, reach, human resources, and sheer institutional presence of churches, so they must be mobilized and equipped to respond to HIV/AIDS in their communities.[28]

The good news is that in many contexts across Asia, Latin America, and Africa, U.S. development efforts have partnered with local religious actors. One reason that many in USAID's field operations are sensitive to engaging religious actors is because 75 percent of the agency's 8,000 employees are foreign nationals, many of whom are rooted in religious societies and may be people of faith themselves. A quick scan of USAID's activities demonstrates how the agency works with local implementing partners who are effective and trusted by the local populace:

- Saving key cultural sites such as a historic mosque in Cyprus, and engaging both the Greek and Turkish communities in the rebuilding process.
- Collaborating with Ethiopian religious leaders on family planning curriculum, child and maternal health, nutrition, and sanitation.
- Helping imams in Mali, through the PEPFAR initiative, to advocate for family planning and HIV/AIDS prevention.
- Sponsoring workshops on restorative justice, with the help of religious leaders like Archbishop Desmond Tutu, to facilitate in the justice and reintegration of former rebel and paramilitary members in Colombia.
- Cooperating with religious leaders who issued *fatwas* promoting polio vaccinations in Nigeria and Indonesia.

Fourth, a challenge for the United States is its lack of government-wide standards for engaging faith-based actors in global development work. As noted in Chapter 2, recent studies, most notably the Center for Strategic and International Studies' *Mixed Blessings* (2007) and the Chicago Council on Global Affairs' *Engaging Religious Communities Abroad* (2010) articulate deep concern that U.S. government officials working in the developing world feel constrained and fearful that such activities are not condoned by Washington. A former U.S. government official reported that although the United States routinely engages religious actors in every area of economic development work, this cooperation is consistently downplayed in reporting to Washington lest it raise controversy about church–state separation. Others noted that although the Bush Administration advanced such issues with its focus on leveling the playing field for faith-based organizations, nonetheless the approach within the bureaucracies of U.S. departments and agencies is inconsistent, with perhaps the greatest latitude being practiced by the U.S. military in engaging with religious actors in Afghanistan and Iraq, and significant reluctance at the Department of State.

One approach is that of USAID, which under the Bush Administration implemented guidelines for working with faith-based organizations that are no longer publicly available on the agency's website.[29] The U.S. government would make the work of foreign assistance much easier if standardized; simple guidelines such as those of USAID were utilized across the board and if each and every case did not have to run a seemingly endless but inconsistent gauntlet of internal legal opinion. However, there has been significant confusion since the Obama Administration has taken office, with a new White House Religious Advisory Council retreading this issue and many of USAID's program notes and updates on working with faith-based organizations disappearing from its website.

United States Agency for International Development
Working with Faith-based Organizations

The United States Agency for International Development (USAID) has more than twenty years of experience in partnering with faith-based organizations conducting humanitarian and development programs overseas. In fact, faith-based PVOs are among USAID's prominent development and relief partners whose technical and institutional capacity has been strengthened through USAID capacity-building grants and through funding of their field activities.

Faith-based PVOs are afforded the opportunity by USAID to compete for funding for humanitarian and social services activities on equal footing with secular PVOs. USAID will not, however, support activities with a significant religious/proselytizing purpose or content. Moreover, all faith-based PVOs are required by USAID to maintain separate accounts for funds to be used for development and humanitarian activities supported by the USG and funds to be used for religious or church-related activities. Similarly, faith-based PVOs are required to ensure adequate and sufficient separation of their religious activities from USG-financed secular activities so as to avoid the appearance that government assistance subsidizes or endorses religion or promotes religious doctrines.

(Continued)

> Consistent with the Establishment Clause of the First Amendment, USAID may finance only programs that have a secular purpose and which do not have the primary effect of advancing or inhibiting religion. This means that a USAID-financed activity may not (1) result in government indoctrination of religion, (2) define its recipients by reference to religion, or (3) create an excessive government entanglement with religion. Assistance recipients must allocate USAID funds on the basis of neutral, secular criteria that neither favor nor disfavor religion, and such assistance must be made available to both religious and secular beneficiaries on a nondiscriminatory basis.
>
> **—From the USAID website; accessed February 2009.**

Fifth, engaging religious actors in development will involve some controversy and disagreement. The U.S. government should expect this and move forward. There are some issues in international development that are flashpoints for conflict between secular and religious approaches. Historically, secular development actors—working on behalf of governments or international organizations—focused exclusively on economic development and disregarded religious groups. In contrast, faith-inspired efforts tended to focus on a holistic notion of human development and were skeptical of secular efforts.[30]

Today, faith-based and secular practitioners are far more aware of one another, and on some issues there can be misunderstanding or disagreement. An example of this is "reproductive health," a catch-all category that potentially includes a wide variety of activities including abstinence training, contraceptive distribution, maternal health education, information on birth spacing, HIV/AIDS prevention, and abortion services. Issues of sex are sensitive and contested within and among religious communities and thus such issues are flashpoints for controversy; both within local communities, but also in U.S. politics as religious, ethical, scientific, and other perspectives weigh in. This makes development work awkward and confrontational, and can result in serious mistrust between those who take different sides on the issues, particularly because all sides define the stakes in terms of valuing human life.

Other controversies exist, such as concerns about proselytization and Establishment Clause issues as noted previously in the Indonesia case. However, this does not mean that the United States should not engage the hot issues, but rather that it should do so in full consultation with the important actors involved, taking seriously the local and religious sentiments of the host population. In short, like all of the issues of religion and foreign policy in this book, these are thorny, complicated issues that should not be avoided because they are difficult. Rather, the world is compelled to engage the issues because they are so complex. The bottom line is that U.S. leadership is vital and America needs to continue collaborative leadership in socioeconomic development and examine the nexus of religion and development so that the opportunities for positive alliances can make a positive impact.

CHAPTER 8

America's Comparative Advantage: Religious Capital

The United States faces an uncertain future in a volatile world. One of the dimensions of that world, or better, one of the multidimensional realities of that world is religion. Religious factors imbue some of the United States' most pressing challenges; religious issues complicate some already testy international relationships. Religious actors are among the country's greatest active threats, and it is disquieting how often the geography of our vital interests coincides with highly religious societies that our foreign policy structures are not prepared to deal with.

The previous chapters have cited numerous other studies, reports, and books from America's finest strategic thinkers. Although there are many things they disagree on, they tend to agree on several critical threats to U.S. interests over the next quarter century: Islamist terrorism, which would be particularly destructive if WMDs were employed; the possible disintegration of the nuclear-armed Pakistani state and subsequent regional chaos; instability on the African continent—including that between Protestants and Muslims—that would make rare raw materials impossible to access; Iranian belligerence or other mass violence in the Middle East, resulting not only in bloodshed but stopping the flow of oil; a militarily aggressive China in the Far East provoking an arms race with its neighbors; a revanchist Russia attempting to destabilize Europe; global pandemic; and environmental degradation accelerated by population growth, ecological damage, and global warming.

Many of these challenges have a religious dimension, either for good or ill. However, if religion is in some way a part of the problem, then at the very least it is in the U.S. interest to try to understand the religious factors involved. Likewise, if religious actors, religious arguments, or religious impulses can provide solutions, then again it is in the U.S. interest to at the very minimum have some appreciation regarding the possibilities. Indeed, if it is true that this short list of challenges are among the gravest external threats faced by a twenty-first century United States, then actually there is hope: the United States is best placed among

Western nations to draw from its deep reservoirs of religious capital to enhance the religious literacy of its foreign policy experts, expand its knowledge resources and capacity on religious issues, and mobilize the full range of actors—both religious and nonreligious, government and nongovernmental—on behalf of peace and security. As the United States faces a highly religious world, it must develop a religiously literate approach to foreign policy that can understand and engage it.

Resurgent Religion in the Twenty-first Century

This book began with the observation, supported by countless empirical studies, that a resurgence of religion is transforming international relations. This resurgence is evidenced in at least five different yet overlapping vectors. These trends are important because they call for a level of religious literacy to understand their significance for U.S. foreign policy. First, individual religious identification and practice is on the rise in many places, such as in Eastern Europe where individuals and collectives reengaged their faith heritage now that the Communism state is safely abolished. This rising religiosity is one of the causes of the second trend: the public expression of religion is increasing. This is most obvious in the greater Middle East, where secular nationalism of various forms began an ignominious retreat, following the Iranian Revolution. That retreat has become a rout as public expression of religion—through political parties, religious justifications for policy, and public demonstrations of personal faith— has come to motivate and infuse the politics of greater Muslim world.

A third trend is "the demise of the state," as termed by globalization theorists and development experts. While the "state" is in decline relative to its privileged position in previous generations, developing governments have always been fragile and the political boundaries of postcolonial entities are often arbitrary recipes for conflict is inconsequential. It is often religious actors within the country that are vital service providers as well as alternative centers of legitimacy and authority. Indeed, as noted in the previous chapter, Rwanda's handful of post-genocide clinics and hospitals are largely run by religious organizations; without them there would be very little healthcare available outside Kigali. It is religious voices, like senior clerics in Indonesia, Grand Ayatollah Ali Sistani in Iraq, or Catholic priests in Central America, who have an immediate, engaged listening audience when they make pronouncements on the issues of the day.

Fourth, religious actors, themes, and movements are increasingly and vigorously transnational. European satirical cartoons about the Prophet Muhammad inflamed Muslim passions worldwide and resulted in threats and attacks on journalists in The Netherlands and mass rioting across the Muslim world. Both al Qaeda and evangelical missionary enterprises utilize international money transfers, preach through the internet, and "franchise" their organizations across state borders. Concepts like "the universal church" and the *ummah* combine with technology, transportation, and global communications to expand the reach and voice of religion across borders.

The fifth observation is the power of religion to motivate individuals and groups in ways that are inexplicable to econometric rational actor models. How does one explain the sacrificial lifestyle of Gandhi? The choice of a suicide bomber? The impetus for charity by the Aga Khan Foundation, Islamic Relief, World Vision, and other faith-based organizations? The decision to risk hardship to serve others as a missionary in China or nurse AIDS orphans in Mozambique?

A sophomoric approach to history might suggest that religion was "lost" during the ideological twentieth century, with the great struggles involving Nazism, Communism, democracy, and capitalism. However, religion was never lost during that period; it was simply rediscovered as a critical factor in international life at Cold War's end when Western social scientists and foreign policy experts were confounded time and again by the intractability of ethnoreligious conflict and the reappearance of claims to kin-, culture-, and religious-based identity in Bosnia, Lebanon, Sudan, Central Asia, East Timor and elsewhere.

Moreover, serious scholarship recognizes that religion did play a strategic role throughout the ideological struggles of the past century. Hitler knew that the national church was a necessary ally, or dangerous threat, so he co-opted it, rooting out religious "threats" like martyred pastors Martin Niemöller and Diedrich Bonhoeffer. Despite public bluster that Christianity was a superstition that would die of its own contradictions, Stalin, Mao, and their successors worked tirelessly to persecute and prosecute those of religious faith, because they realized that religious faith was an intellectual and spiritual threat to their programs. Saddam Hussein understood this, jailing or executing senior Shia clerics who criticized his regime, yet later promoted himself as "Defender of the Faith" in order to rally religious support in Iraq and across the region. Washington and its allies likewise understood the potency of religion and used it as a rallying point in Poland and across the Arab world against atheistic Communism.[1]

Beyond these instrumental approaches to religion, the more important fact of the twentieth century is that the lived religion of billions of citizens, from Dallas to Sao Paolo to Nairobi to Kandahar to Manila to Cape Town, was always there; its global and political significance was simply neglected by most scholars and policy elites. Chapters 3 and 4 demonstrated that this neglect was largely rooted in the secularist bias of the educational establishment and government elites. The prevailing understanding of modernization from the 1950s until the present is that countries that effectively modernize tend to secularize. More specifically, modernization theory expected that science, education, and rising standards of living due to modern "advances" would naturally cause a population to leave the superstitious, patriarchal, and hierarchical legacy of religion behind in favor of the materialistic consumer society. Generations of diplomats and scholars, drunk at the well of modernization theory, were totally unprepared for religious identities, religious actors, and faith-based organizations to rise to prominence with the fall of the international relations architecture at the Cold War's end. Indeed, it is only in the past few years that scholars are beginning to adjust and rewrite the paradigms of IR theory, rooted in realism and liberal internationalism, to account for these global realities.

Chapters 5 and 6 argued that adding religion to the palette of international affairs thinking does not mean throwing out everything else; it means a more vibrant and realistic portrayal of the world. Certainly the traditional studies of economics and the national interest still have a role to play, but religious literacy can help refine notions of how culture and religion influence collective identity, a society's valuing of money and resources, and definitions of national interests. So too, the paradigms of realism and liberal internationalism can remain true to their core tenets—power and cooperation—by widening their vistas to take into account nongovernmental authority and power and the role of faith-based claims and organizations to encourage, or thwart, cooperation on behalf of peace.

The heart of this book, therefore, is the call for a religiously literate foreign policy, one that puts aside the secularist bias of the past and takes into account the religious factors already present in thoughtful analyses of global issues, most notably those of war and peace. Indeed, any intelligent evaluation of the impetus for American foreign policy legacies, such as human rights advocacy or the ethical underpinnings of democracy, must encounter theological and faith-based actors and justifications. In short, a review of U.S. domestic and foreign policy history would find religion to be ever present in the public debate; and such should continue as part of the larger tapestry in the future.

This is not to say that religion is "everything" in U.S. politics and foreign policy; the goal of this book is to counter the prevailing trend that religion should be "nothing": that it is too dangerous, too complicated, too inflammatory, too unscientific, or downright unconstitutional for study and engagement. This is the central argument of the book, that a wise, effective twenty-first century U.S. foreign policy must be religiously literate, in the same way Americans expect their diplomatic corps to have some literacy in economics, political-military issues, development, and security concerns. The United States is well-placed to lead the West in this arena, not because the government is religiously literate (yet), but due to the high level of religious capital within American society. The United States many of the ingredients for a religiously literate foreign policy: a knowledgeable public, some scholarly expertise, and the wisdom and expertise of traditional and Track 2 diplomats.

America's Comparative Advantage: Domestic Religious Capital

This dilemma of how to understand and engage highly religious communities around the globe is being faced, or avoided, in every Western capital today. The good news is that the United States is better equipped to deal with the global resurgence of religion than most. Few countries can match Americans' distinctive religious capital—those human and intellectual resources that can provide expertise and wisdom on religious dynamics in a variety of disciplines. Alexis de Tocqueville observed:

> Religion in America takes no direct part in the government of society, but it must be regarded as the first of their political institutions. I do not know whether all Americans have a sincere faith and religion, for who can search the human heart? But I am certain that they hold it to be indispensable to the maintenance of republican institutions. This opinion is not peculiar to a class of citizens or to a party, but it belongs to the whole nation and to every rank of society.[2]

The American experience should provide a uniquely deep appreciation for the role that religion plays in culture, society, and politics and thus provide American government representatives—at home and abroad—a rich array of domestic resources from which to draw. That capital is vital to U.S. foreign policy when it engages a religious world, and should provide the United States with a comparative advantage over its secular Western European counterparts when it interacts with religious societies in Latin America, Asia, Africa, Eastern Europe, and the greater Middle East.

The United States abounds in religious resources, including its religious society. Survey data continue to report that the vast majority of Americans believe in God, identify with a religious tradition, point to times in their life when faith took on increased salience, and believe that religion has a place in the public sphere. In comparison to our allies, a recent global survey indicated that an average U.S. citizen is more than twice as likely to be "very religious" as a German and about three times as likely as someone from Russia, France, Britain, Australia, Spain, or Japan.[3]

Second, the United States has a diverse population, varied in ethnicity, culture, and religion. As President Obama observed in his inaugural address, "We know that our patchwork heritage is a strength, not a weakness. We are a nation of Christians and Muslims, Jews and Hindus—and non-believers." America has citizen representatives of every religious group within its borders, meaning that Americans have a wealth of local expertise on many of the key issues of faith around the world. This should provide the United States with enormous advantages in this newly defined global context, and yet, the United States continues to trip over itself in appropriately integrating religious awareness into foreign policy. Those representing the world's religions—some of whom are recent immigrants to the United States—should provide valuable insight to U.S. government officials, and yet they are often held at arm's length. America's diverse population suggests that if the government does its job well, it will attract individuals with a variety of talents and expertise—including in matters of culture, religion, and language—to public service.

Of equal importance are the messages that immigrants and religious communities broadcast informally to their co-religionists and family members abroad about their American experience and their ability to worship freely in the United States. Recent survey data provide an insight into religious diversity and opportunity in the United States. A Gallup study titled "Muslim Americans: A National Portrait" released in March 2009 indicated that 80 percent of Muslims in the United States state that religion is "very important" to them. Unlike Muslim-majority societies such as Saudi Arabia, the study indicated that Muslim women "are roughly equal to men in education, income, and mosque attendance" and that the Muslim population in the United States has high rates of education and employment.[4]

Freedom and opportunity for religious minorities is true for other groups as well. According to the Pew Forum's 2007 U.S. Religious Landscape Survey,

> Nearly half of Hindus in the United States, one-third of Jews and a quarter of Buddhists have obtained postgraduate education, compared with only about one-in-ten of the adult population overall. Hindus and Jews are also much more likely than other groups to report high income levels.[5]

In short, American society blends the social, political, and material liberties known as the American dream and it is characterized by the robust religious devotion of some segments of the American public in a day-to-day environment of pluralism where people of faith, agnostics, and atheists live together harmoniously.

A third feature of American religious capital is that the U.S. government can call upon the religious, cultural, and professional expertise of Americans who have served in foreign contexts with business, NGOs, and faith-based organizations. A great American strength has been its willingness to accept tourists and immigrants as well as American citizens' interest in traveling and living abroad. Hence, there is a cadre of individuals with professional expertise in foreign environments who may be useful in government service or consulted with in order to provide the very best religious and cultural understanding.

Private individuals with foreign experience from outside government are particularly important in an era when the U.S. government has a heightened awareness of the safety of its representatives abroad, and where American diplomats, aid workers, and even military personnel spend less and less time outside of the embassy or beyond "the wire." For instance, the U.S. ambassador to an Asian country was recently briefed on local social conditions by the head of a major Western faith-based humanitarian organization because the organization has a human presence on the ground in hundreds of villages where there is no presence of the United States or host governments.

Fourth, significant resources exist at American universities and think tanks to aid in understanding religious and cultural dynamics. Although much of American higher education is highly secularized—with some sectors antagonistic to religion—America remains the world's most important intellectual center, including in the nexus of religion, culture, and society. It is to American universities, research institutes, and intelligentsia that the U.S. government can also turn for assistance on the complicated and diverse issues that religion touches: economic development, service provision in postconflict societies, religious sources of terrorism, faith-based peacemaking, religious nuances of culture and diplomacy, and religious language in foreign political narratives.

The academy has not been entirely idle on these issues, particularly in the wake of ethnoreligious violence in the 1990s and the 9/11 attacks. Major research initiatives on religion's relationship to politics, violence, and peace have been undertaken at a variety of prestigious universities including Georgetown, Notre Dame, and Columbia; at organizations such as the Council on Foreign Relations, the Chicago Council on Global Affairs, and the Center for Strategic and International Studies in Washington, D.C.; and with the support of foundations, most notably the Henry R. Luce Foundation and the John Templeton Foundation. However, have American universities taken up Stephen Prothero's challenge, discussed in Chapter 6, to develop a baseline of religious literacy when teaching their undergraduate students? There is little evidence of a systematic shift in this direction in higher education.

Another area where the United States has a religious comparative advantage over many Western countries is its tradition of respecting religious freedom at home and abroad. A variety of factors noted above, from the absence of a state-ordained religion to a vibrant religious pluralism to legacies of immigration, make the American experience quite different from that of Europe. Historically, most European countries have state religions with checkered histories when it comes to religious toleration, ironically causing the public to increasingly see religion as irrelevant. Some of the highly secularized European governments, notably France and Turkey, have severely circumscribed the religious sphere, causing outrage among some sectors. That resentment is broadcast worldwide on a daily basis to co-religionists via the media and personal communications.

In contrast, the American experience of little government interference in the realm of faith has resulted in a rich tapestry of individual and collective religious practice. Moreover, religious groups have been free to broadly participate in the larger marketplace of ideas and activities that constitute civil society, solving collective action problems and contributing to social capital. Political scientist Alfred Stepan calls this the "twin tolerations": mutual accommodation and respect between the political and religious institutions of an open society.[6] When Americans carefully consider their past, they recognize that this is an area of development and imperfect advancement at many points in American history, but revel in how religious liberty and its attendant freedoms—speech, conscience, assembly, and press—are firmly entrenched today. The United States is committed to a similar level of freedom for people everywhere, even though this commitment is sometimes misunderstood in foreign capitals.

Finally, American religious capital is part of the foundation of U.S. support for human rights and development; conceptions of human worth and helping others have been influenced by faith for much of American history and to many of its citizens. Furthermore, religious voices continue to be major players at home and abroad, including in passing recent legislation against human trafficking, condemning North Korean human rights abuses, and supporting international religious freedom. Religious voices have partnered with secular human rights advocates in calling upon the conscience of the nation regarding genocide, religious persecution behind Eastern Europe's Iron Curtain and East Asia's Bamboo Curtain, and most recently in issues of maltreatment and torture of enemy combatants by representatives of the U.S. government. Publics around the world look to the United States for leadership on these issues, a critical part of American public diplomacy, democracy advancement, and human rights initiatives.

American leadership is instrumental in humanitarian assistance, human security, and economic development as well. The United States has long been a major government donor to those in need around the world, but it is the robust voluntary giving of the American people, often through their houses of worship or faith-based organizations, that distinguishes the United States from other Western countries. Moreover, Americans are known to be both curious and caring, with tens of thousands streaming out of the country each year to provide aid and respite via short-term missions trips, semesters abroad to participate in development work, and other avenues of service to others. Not only is this the unofficial face of America, but it is a source of religious and cultural understanding that enriches the nation's religious capital.

In sum, the U.S. government represents a public where people of varied faiths and no faith live in harmony, and the U.S. government has at its fingertips almost limitless resources for developing a wise and nuanced understanding of the religious and cultural contexts which it engages around the world daily and can draw from its own experience of religious freedom and pluralism. Therefore, it is disappointing that the United States has not done a better job in forecasting the role of religion in societies from Poland to Iran to the Philippines, and America endangers its national security when it fails to grasp the risks and possibilities posed by religious dynamics in places like Afghanistan, Nigeria, and Colombia.

Putting Religious Literacy and Religious Capital to Work

Understanding the religious dimension of societies and international affairs is critical to American diplomacy, for without literacy and wisdom in this area, the United States will continue to misread some dynamics of international affairs, will obliviously offend some societies, and will strain to comprehend phenomena and explanations that can only be apprehended by considering religious variables. Alternately, the United States could take seriously the religious identities and motivations of foreign societies (just as it considers their economic motives), respectfully engage a wider range of major social actors in foreign publics (those with real local legitimacy, including legitimacy based on faith), modify and/or expand the training of foreign affairs experts on the religious dimensions of foreign policy, and recalibrate its public diplomacy strategies for a world experiencing a resurgence of religion in both the life of individuals and corporately across societies. Which will it be? If the United States learns anything from observing the past quarter century, it should be the salience of religion to individual and collective identity and the increased infusion of religious actors and narratives in political discourse. The United States has learned some lessons; and a wide variety of disparate, disconnected, ad hoc, short-term initiatives across a number of federal departments and agencies suggest that there are entrepreneurs within the government who take the global resurgence of religion seriously and want to engage it appropriately. Sustained, systematic, whole-of-government and whole-of-society efforts are needed to take advantage of opportunities and confront challenges. When the United States has done this well, it has largely been due to a high level of religious sensitivity and literacy by an individual, often a result of that person's private or family faith tradition.

The most typical examples of successful religiously literate diplomacy are those based on *personal initiative*. Former U.S. Ambassador to Qatar Joseph Ghougassian was a person of faith but unprepared for what he found on arrival. He recalls, "I had spent two months in consultations in the Department of State prior to arriving in Qatar, and the lack of religious freedom had never been hinted at." Qatar, like Saudi Arabia, allowed no religious practice other than Islam within its borders at the time—not even for foreign nationals and diplomats. Ghougassian continues,

> the crux of the matter, however, was how to change the minds and hearts of the Qatari officials without offending their sensitivities and sensibilities...I would not act as a colonial agent, but rather...with humility, astuteness, and in total friendship with my interlocutors.

Ambassador Ghougassian promoted U.S. ideals *and* U.S. interests successfully in Qatar and developed many relationships with key national figures. Ultimately, Qatar allowed Christian worship services to occur, and two decades later, religious toleration is now enshrined in Qatar's constitution and other faiths may practice there.[7]

Personal initiative matters today. The relationships developed by U.S. government representatives with their foreign counterparts, be it the American Chairman of the Joint Chiefs of Staff with his Pakistani counterpart or the U.S. ambassador to Nigeria with the major Muslim and Christian leaders therein, are a critical part of U.S. foreign policy. Such relationships need not be entirely ad hoc: the U.S. government should make it routine practice for embassy officials to seek out and build relationships with the major social actors in a society, which will include imams, pastors, priests, and the leaders of faith-based organizations in religious societies throughout much of the world.

Other tangible ways that a new approach to religion in U.S. foreign policy can pay dividends is in *interreligious engagement*. Unfortunately the U.S. blundered terribly in its lack of a coherent approach to issues of religion and culture in Iraq following the 2003 invasion, but after years of errors the United States began to see breakthroughs for peace and security through interreligious dialogue and the engagement of religious figures. Perhaps the most important example of "getting religion right" in Iraq was the 2007 Iraqi Inter-Religious Congress discussed in Chapter 6, which occurred in tandem with the U.S. military "surge" and the Sunni "Awakening," helping stem the tide of Iraq's descent into civil war. Military chaplains may have a unique role to play, such as in this report from Afghanistan:

> The Afghans [ANA soldiers] observed the chaplain's support to the American soldiers and wanted their own chaplain. They elected a young mullah (Muslim clergy) to act as their chaplain. The Mullah contacted Chaplain E—for help. Using materials from his Chaplain's Officer Basic Course, altered by him to meet the need, he first discussed the concept of pluralism. This became a key issue that led to successful training and a strategic secondary effect. The Mullah became so positively excited about the use of pluralism within this military chaplain context, that he returned to his madrassa (religious school) in Pakistan to tell folks there of his experience. According to [the] CENTCOM operations chaplain, the mullah said, "Americans are all right. The information about these folks we've been receiving is wrong. They're good people."[8]

A third way that taking religion seriously can happen in U.S. foreign policy is by *directly engaging religious actors* in the critical debates of international life, such as democracy and human rights. A recent example of this is the effort to reinforce democracy in Indonesia. From 1997 to 2007 the U.S. government funded a program implemented by The Asia Foundation called "Islam and Civil Society." The goal of the program, as it was initially envisioned, was to "strengthen the efforts of a diverse group of Muslim religious NGOs who were committed to promoting the engagement of Indonesia's Muslim majority population in building democracy and civil society."[9] This novel cluster of programs included civic education and the development of a course book titled Democracy, Human Rights, and Civil Society used on over 80 university campuses, democracy workshops for preachers (*khatib*), radio programs on pluralism and Islam, training seminars for women preachers (*muballighat*) on women's social and political rights, and professionalization training for political parties. The "Islam and Civil Society" program was designed to engage a religious society by aiding the transition away from the traditions of authoritarian politics associated with the Suharto era as well as counter the ideology of violent religious extremists. After a decade of work and tens of thousands of people touched, the program ended in 2007.

The United States is generally welcomed when it helps people. The work of economic and political development is too great for any one government or institution to handle, so *the U.S. must find partners, many of whom are religiously inspired or faith-based*. In spite of many challenges, USAID has partnered with many faith-based service providers, often in remote or primitive conditions, to positively impact human lives around the world. A few examples of that work conclude this chapter, including:

- Working with religious charities to help abandoned children in Romania.
- Engaging religious actors in tandem with other leaders on environmental issues in the Philippines, resulting in religiously and culturally informed environmental law.
- Training imams in Bangladesh on development problems such as family health, early childhood education, agriculture, and human rights.
- Working with local sheikhs in rural Yemen to develop "women's councils" where women and girls can learn new skills and about health issues.

Finally, *Track 2 diplomacy will often support or reinforce U.S. government priorities*. The traditional "track" of diplomacy (Track 1) is official government-to-government relations. Hence, those who speak of alternate tracks generally mean non-governmental actors engaging governments directly (sometimes called Track 1.5) or individuals without government credentials (Track 2) working to diminish suspicion and build trust (diplomacy) across barriers of region, race, or religion. For this book's purposes, both types of diplomacy, as they are led by individuals with no current government credentials, fall under the rubric of Track 2.

The notion of Track 2 diplomacy is largely associated with the efforts of faith-based actors. True, representatives of secular NGOs and other organizations may engage in consultations in pursuit of peace and understanding, but it is largely religious individuals and organizations that have pioneered the concept of Track 2 diplomacy. Track 2 diplomacy relies heavily on the notion that in societies riven by conflict, be it internally or externally, faith-based diplomacy can work quietly and unobtrusively to build trust, dispel misperceptions, and nurture relationships. One can easily imagine a dozen or more different types of scenarios wherein Track 2 "diplomats" have a role to play: as sounding boards for traditional diplomats about conditions "on the ground," as background experts for government agencies on both sides of a conflict, in arranging off-the-record meetings between the leaders of parties in conflict, in serving as mediators or third-party arbitrators in delicate situations, as "trainers" on the topics of peace and security, as subject matter experts who can explain the United States (or other countries') position on contested issues (e.g., religious freedom policy), as back-channels for communication among belligerents, as moral entrepreneurs willing to reach out to the leaders of communities in conflict on behalf of peace, and as nongovernmental champions for policy change (e.g., human rights).

One example is Robert Seiple, founder of the Institute of Global Engagement (IGE). Seiple spent much of his career in higher education and as the president of World Vision, the largest private relief and development organization in the world. Seiple spent 2 years as the United States' first ever Ambassador-at-Large for International Religious Freedom at the U.S. State Department, after which he founded IGE. Seiple's global contacts, from both before and during his time at the State Department, have made him unusually qualified to serve as a Track 2 diplomat, particularly on issues of religious freedom. He has written about those experiences in a variety of places, including his book *Ambassadors of Hope* and in IGE's journal, the *Review of Faith and International Affairs*. One example of his work is that while serving as Ambassador-at-Large for International Religious Freedom, Seiple cultivated relationships with the senior leadership of Laos. A traditionally Buddhist-majority country tightly controlled by a Communist military regime since 1975, Laos (like its neighbors) has been frigid toward Western human rights and religious freedom advocacy. However, as Seiple describes it, over a series of meetings that began while he was in government but that continued after he was out of government, Seiple developed personal relationships with senior Laotian officials and persuaded them that it was in their interest to lessen their persecution of people of faith, particularly—but not exclusively— Christians. Seiple recounts how upon leaving the State Department he founded an NGO called the Institute for Global Engagement, and through it he stayed in direct contact with Laos, including hosting a high level Laotian delegation in the United States. Following that visit, 34 of 37 Christians in prison were released and a new religious freedom decree was declared. In 2004, the State Department's International Religious Freedom report noted that only two countries had experienced improvement on religious freedom: one of them was Laos. The approach is what Seiple and his son, current IGE President Chris Seiple, have called "relational diplomacy," building mutually respectful relationships that are aware of difference and which seek to demonstrate the overlap between moral imperatives and national and national interests.[10]

A related approach to Track 2 diplomacy is occurring in Pakistan's madrassas. Douglas Johnston, founder of the International Center for Religion and Development (ICRD), leads the effort and is the foremost voice on faith-based diplomacy. His co-authored book, *Religion, The Missing Dimension of Statecraft* was followed shortly thereafter by his *Faith-Based Diplomacy: Trumping Realpolitik*—they remain the foundational works in calling for religious literacy in the foreign policy establishment and in pointing to religious opportunities for peace. Johnston, a former senior defense department official, Harvard PhD, retired Navy Reserve Officer, and past Executive Vice President of the Center for Strategic and International Studies, founded ICRD to "address identity-based conflicts that exceed the reach of traditional diplomacy by incorporating religion as part of the solution. More often than not, these take the form of ethnic conflict, tribal warfare, or religious hostilities. "Thus, ICRD has been engaged in some of the world's most dangerous conflicts, most notably Kashmir and the internal turbulence along the borders of Afghanistan and Pakistan, with the goal of "linking religious reconciliation with official or unofficial diplomacy, [to create] a new synergy for peacemaking that serves both of these needs."

A case in point is ICRD's work in madrassa reform in Pakistan. Madrassas have made headlines in the West as the incubators of Islamic terrorism due to the reactionary, pietistic approach of many madrassas. In fact, madrassas are often the only form of education available to the poor, as they provide a rudimentary religious education and a hot meal for many of the students. The Pakistani government has been at a loss for years about how to deal with madrassas: they have deep local legitimacy in many communities, they provide a service—however rudimentary—that is often not available from the government, and at times they have been supportive of government policies. However, the madrassa system has increasingly been seen as destabilizing by many national leaders, both in Islamabad and in the West.

In this milieu, beginning in 2003 ICRD began an outreach initiative to Pakistani madrassas, developing relationships with religious educators as well as state-funded teachers and university professors. Over the years, ICRD's relationships have grown as they have hired Pakistanis to lead the local work, and as the organization has worked alongside madrassa leaders to introduce modern resources and curriculum, particularly in the social and hard sciences, to the classroom. At the same time, ICRD has winsomely stressed the tolerant and pluralistic aspects of Islam as appropriate for madrassa instruction. A study of the ICRD program, commissioned by the Smith Richardson Foundation, reported,

> ICRD's Pakistan Madrassa Project "came at an excellent time in a context and process of change and is very relevant as it addresses an urgent need in

Pakistan." In addition to the improvement of teaching methods (pedagogical aspects of the training), the ICRD project is one of the very few madrassa programs "that directly focuses on themes of human rights, democracy, women rights, inter- and intra-faith dialogue, and conflict resolution [sic].... [The project] is absolutely relevant to the existing needs and wants of the madrassa leaders."[11]

ICRD's work has been publicly endorsed by both Pakistan's National Madrassa Oversight Board and retired General Ehsan ul-Haq, former Chair of Pakistan's Joint Chiefs of Staff and, before that, Director of Inter-Services Intelligence (ISI).

With the work of ICRD, IGE, and other Track 2 organizations in mind, it is worthwhile to reflect on the nexus of Track 2 diplomacy and U.S. interests. It is hard to imagine that Ambassador Seiple and his IGE staff are not consulted by U.S. government officials regarding his most recent travels and points of contact, particularly in IGE's priority countries of Vietnam, Laos, and Pakistan; the same likely holds true with regard to Douglas Johnston and ICRD's priority countries: Pakistan, Kashmir, Afghanistan, Iran, Sudan, and the Middle East. These organizations have contacts where no U.S. official can go (e.g., Iran) and move far beyond the official channels in the constrained environments of Ho Chi Minh City or Khartoum. It is entirely possible that foreign governments and foreign actors send signals via Track 2 diplomats to Western governments in discreet ways. Track 2 diplomats can forge long-standing relationships over a period of years, or even decades, whereas U.S. diplomats have a way of moving on to their next post rather quickly—embassy teams often move annually (as does the U.S. military) in "hardship" posts like Kabul, Herat, Islamabad, and parts of Africa. Moreover, the credibility of Track 2 diplomats is based not on the throw weight of their nation's military, but their hosts' perception that they are acting in accord with the tenets of their faith and in the spirit of friendship and brotherly regard. Finally, if ICRD continues to be successful in supporting madrassa reform, or if IGE's outreach to Laos bears fruit for the religious liberties of its minority groups, it is beneficial to U.S. foreign policy interests, even if it is not directly supported by the U.S. government.

Conclusion

Although this book is nearing its end, for America this can be a new beginning. This book, in tandem with the calls of other scholars and some recent think tank reports, is a challenge to the United States and allied governments, to their citizens, and to the academic community. It is a call to reflect, commit, and act on behalf of a sophisticated, successful, religiously literate U.S. foreign policy. It can be done.

For the U.S. government, Chapter 6 identified four main points of action. First, the Administration needs to clarify the domain of government engagement of religion in its overseas relations. This is largely a task distinct from the culture wars at home; it is clearly the purview of the Executive Branch and there is a long, albeit unwritten, history of U.S. diplomacy in highly religious contexts. Such "clarification" would be liberating for many in the foreign aid and diplomatic communities, and it would essentially put them on the same footing as Defense Department personnel, who frankly worry far less about whether or not they are violating the Establishment Clause when engaging highly religious publics.

The U.S. government must also rapidly increase the knowledge resources available to its personnel and at the same time invest over the long-term in a deeper set of capabilities and assets on religion and culture, from academic experts and programming at U.S. government learning centers to a cadre of specialists available at embassies and defense headquarters worldwide. Finally, the government needs a national strategy for engaging a highly religious world, a strategy that takes into account the tough questions like the following: How and when does the United States engage Islamists like Egypt's Muslim Brotherhood, elected Hamas, and elected Hezbollah? Develop relationships with influential clerics, such as the Sistanis of the world? Counter the religious narratives that challenge American commitments to international security and human rights, be they from Colombia's ELN, Uganda's Lord's Resistance Army, or Pakistan's Lashkar-e-Taiba? Support religious narratives for security and justice, be it from an Afghan jirga or Archbishop Desmond Tutu or Burmese monks? How does America do public diplomacy better to counter enemy narratives and simultaneously champion American values in the war of ideas?

However, this is not just the work of the State Department or the National Security Council, although many of their most recent senior leaders have avoided these questions over the past 2 years. These topics should also motivate action from civil society, both religious and nonreligious, as well as houses of worship, scholars, students, and concerned lay people. Moreover, there is much to be done in the scholarly community. Indeed, Chapters 4 and 5 suggest a great deal of opportunity for rising scholars on these issues. Traditional international relations theory paradigms such as realism and liberal internationalism can be stretched, explored, and expanded to develop intellectual resources to help us understand the role of religious phenomena in contemporary international affairs. Scholarship in sociology, political science, anthropology, and comparative politics, to name a few, can help Americans better "map" and understand what is happening both globally and locally in this era of resurgent religion. Strategists and futurists should be analyzing what the implications are for countries like China and Russia should religious pluralism topple the authoritarian monocracies. And there is much to be done to train the next generation of students to better apprehend a world of religious multidimensionality, cultural difference, and linguistic diversity which will make them better citizens of the United States and leaders on the global stage.

Notes

Chapter 1

1. "Taseer's Death Exposes Pakistani Fissures," BBC Online News. Available at: www.bbc.co.uk/news/world-south-asia-12124761 (accessed January 10, 2011).
2. "Salman Taseer: Thousands Mourn Punjab Governor," BBC Online News. January 5, 2011. Available at: www.bbc.co.uk/news/world-south-asia-12116764 (accessed February 1, 2011).
3. The larger results of this survey can be found at: http://pewglobal.org/2007
4. See note 2 above.
5. Jayshree Bajoria, Council on Foreign Relations. "Pakistan's New Generation of Terrorists." Available at: www.cfr.org/pakistan/pakistans-new-generation-terrorists/p15422 (accessed February 7, 2011); Jessica Stern, "The Protean Enemy," *Foreign Affairs,* vol. 82, no. 4 (July–August, 2003), 27–40.
6. Douglas Johnston and Cynthia Sampson, eds, *Religion, the Missing Dimension of Statecraft* (Center for Strategic and International Studies, Washington, DC) (New York: Oxford University Press, 1994).
7. Title of Scott M. Thomas's book, *The Global Resurgence of Religion and the Transformation of International Relations: The Struggle for the Soul of the Twenty-First Century* (New York: Palgrave-Macmillan, 2005).
8. Benjamin Barber, "Jihad vs. McWorld," *The Atlantic Monthly* (March, 1992, 53–61), later a book by the same name (New York: Times Books, 1995).
9. Samuel P. Huntington, *The Third Wave: Democratization in the Late 20th Century* (Norman: University of Oklahoma Press, 1993); "The Clash of Civilizations?" *Foreign Affairs* Vol. 92, No. 3 (Summer, 1993, 22–49); *The Clash of Civilizations and the Remaking of the World Order* (New York: Simon and Schuster, 1998). The response to Huntington was vociferous and, at times, combative. Examples include David A. Welch, "The 'Clash of Civilizations' Thesis as an Argument and as a Phenomenon," *Security Studies,* vol. 6, no. 4 (Summer, 1997, 197–216); Ronald Inglehart and Pippa Norris, "The True Clash of Civilizations," *Foreign Policy* No. 135 (March/April, 2003, 63–70).
10. This definition is adapted from that provided in the American Heritage Dictionary of the English Language, fourth edition (2006).
11. (A) World Values Survey (2002), (B) John Micklethwait and Adrian Woolridge, *God is Back: How the Global Religious Revival is Changing the World* (New York: Penguin, 2009); (C) Ibid.; (D) Pew Global Attitudes Survey (2007).
12. This notion of "lived religion" has wide currency today in comparative religious studies, but was coined in observations of U.S. religious practice by David Hall in *Lived Religion: Toward a History of Practice* (Princeton, NJ: Princeton University Press, 1997).

13. Scott M. Thomas, *The Global Resurgence of Religion*, 26.
14. Philip Jenkins, *The Next Christendom: The Coming of Global Christianity* (Oxford: Oxford University Press, 2002), see chapter 1.
15. José Casanova, *Public Religions in the Modern World* (Chicago, IL: University of Chicago Press, 1994).
16. I acknowledge Dalia Mogahed, co-author with John Esposito of *Who Speaks for Islam? What a Billion Muslims Really Think* (Washington, D.C.: Gallup Press, 2008), for framing this issue in this way.
17. R. Scott Appleby, "Building Sustainable Peace: The Roles of Local and Transnational Religious Actors," in Thomas Banchoff, ed., *Religious Pluralism, Globalization, and World Politics* (Oxford: Oxford University Press, 2008), 125–54.
18. This term is used by Scott Appleby, *The Ambivalence of the Sacred: Religion, Violence and Reconciliation* (Lanham, MD: Rowman and Littlefield, 1999).
19. See www.kiva.org/help/facts (accessed February 12, 2011).
20. "Glocalization" is a term used in numerous books and articles to denote the nexus of globalizing trends with local realities. One example is Thomas L. Friedman's *Hot, Flat, and Crowded: Why We Need a Green Revolution* (New York: Farrar, Straus & Giroux, 2008).
21. Edward Luttwak, "The Missing Dimension," in Johnson and Sampson, eds, *Religion, the Missing Dimension of Statecraft*, 10.
22. Stephen Prothero, *Religious Literacy: What Every American Needs to Know— And Doesn't* (New York: HarperCollins Publishers, 2007), 11–12.

Chapter 2

1. MidEast Web, "Osama Bin Laden's Jihad and Text of Fatwas and Declaration of War." Available at: www.mideastweb.org/osamabinladen1.htm (accessed February 7, 2011).
2. Daniel Philpott, "The Challenge of September 11 to Secularism in International Relations," *World Politics*, vol. 55, no. 1 (2002), 66–95.
3. E. H. Carr, *The Twenty Years' Crisis, 1919–1939* (New York: Palgrave, 2001).
4. Yves Lapid, "The Third Debate: On the Prospects of International Theory in a Post-Positivist Era," *International Studies Quarterly*, vol. 33 (1989), 235–54.
5. Say that there are at least two notable exceptions: Scott Thomas 2004 book and the work of Daniel Philpott.
6. José Casanova, *Public Religions in the Modern World* (Chicago, IL: University of Chicago Press, 1994).
7. Charles Taylor, *A Secular Age* (Cambridge: Harvard University Press, 2007).
8. Elizabeth Shakman Hurd, *The Politics of Secularism in International Relations* (Princeton, NJ: Princeton University Press, 2008). See especially chapter 1.
9. Timothy A. Byrnes and Peter J. Katzenstein, eds, *Religion in an Expanding Europe* (Cambridge University Press, 2006).

10. Eric O. Hanson, *Religion and Politics in the International System Today* (Cambridge: Cambridge University Press, 2006).

11. Pavlos Hatzopoulos and Fabio Petito, eds, *Religion in International Relations: The Return from Exile* (New York and London: Palgrave Macmillan, 2003).

12. Ibid., 33.

13. G. John Ikenberry and Anne-Marie Slaughter, Co-Directors, *Forging a World of Liberty under Law U.S. National Security in the 21st Century: Final Report of the Princeton Project on National Security* (The Woodrow Wilson School of Public and International Affairs) (Princeton, NJ: Princeton University Press, 2006), 13.

14. Ibid., 34.

15. Ibid., 44.

16. National Intelligence Council, *Global Trends 2025: A Transformed World* (Washington, D.C.: Superintendent of Documents, U.S. Government Printing Office, 2005), 24. Available at: http://oai.dtic.mil/oai/oai?verb=getRecord& metadataPrefix=html&identifier=ADA490430 (accessed February 7, 2011).

17. Ibid., xi.

18. Ibid., 86.

19. "State Department Pledges Major Reforms with New QDDR," http://thecable. foreignpolicy.com/posts/2010/12/15/state_department_pledges_major_ reforms_with_new_qddr. Published December 15, 2010 (accessed December 18, 2010).

20. Quadrennial Diplomacy and Development Review, released December 15, 2010, 85. Available at: www.state.gov/documents/organization/153142.pdf

21. Ibid., 121.

22. Ibid., 42.

23. The document's only oblique mention of any of the world's major faith traditions is two references to inviting visitors (e.g., students) to the United States from "the Muslim world."

24. "The National Security Strategy" May 2010 http://www.whitehouse.gov/sites/ default/files/rss_viewer/national_security_strategy.pdf, 13.

25. President Obama's speech to the United Nations, September 23, 2010.

26. Liora Danan and Alice Hunt, *Mixed Blessings: U.S. Government Engagement with Religion in Conflict-Prone Settings* (Washington, D.C.: Center for Strategic and International Studies, 2007), 28.

27. Taken from Robert Ruby and Timothy Samuel Shah, "Nigeria's Presidential Election: The Christian-Muslim Divide," *The Pew Forum on Religion & Public Life* (March 21, 2007).

28. *Changing Course: A New Direction for U.S. Relations with the Muslim World* (Washington, D.C.: Leadership Group on U.S.-Muslim Engagement, 2008), 1.

29. Ibid., 11.

30. Ibid., 19.

Chapter 3

1. Stephen Kinzer, *All the Shah's Men: An American Coup and the Roots of Middle East Terror* (Hoboken, NJ: John Wiley & Sons, Inc., 2008), 196–7.

2. Gary Sick, *All Fall Down: America's Tragic Encounter with Iran* (New York: Penguin Books, 1986).

3. www.mindef.gov.sg/safti/pointer/back/journals/2000/Vol26_4/8.htm (accessed November 11, 2010); Jimmy Carter, *Keeping the Faith: Memoirs of a President* (New York: Bantam Books, 1982), 438; www.kcl.ac.uk/lhcma/summary/xi70-001.shtml (accessed January 5, 2011).

4. New Jersey was originally part of New Amsterdam; when the English took control from the Dutch in 1664, two English colonies resulted: New York and New Jersey.

5. Georgia's charter dates from 1732. Alan Taylor, *American Colonies: The Settling of North America* (New York: Penguin Putnam Inc., 2001); Henry William Elson, *History of the United States of America* (New York: The MacMillan Company, 1904), 210–16: "Chart of the Thirteen Original Colonies."

6. Henk van Nierop, "Similar Problems, Different Outcomes: The Revolt of the Netherlands and the Wars of Religion in France," in Karel Davids and Jan Lucassen, eds, *A Miracle Mirrored: The Dutch Republic in European Perspective* (Cambridge: Cambridge University Press, 1995), 26–56.

7. David D. Hall, ed., *Lived Religion in America: Toward a History of Practice* (Princeton, NJ: Princeton University Press, 1997); Carville Earle, "Pioneers of Providence: The Anglo-American Experience, 1492–1792," *Annals of the Association of American Geographers*, vol. 82, no. 3; Karl W. Butzer, "The Americas before and after 1492: Current Geographical Research, *The Annals of the Association of American Geographers*, vol. 82, no. 3 (September, 1992), 345–68; David G. Hackett, "Sociology of Religion and American Religious History: Retrospect and Prospect," *Journal for the Scientific Study of Religion*, vol. 27, no. 4 (December, 1988), 461–74.

8. Cf. Matthew 5.37.

9. Patricia U. Bonomi, *Under the Cope of Heaven: Religion, Society, and Politics in Colonial America* (New York: Oxford University Press, 1986); Library of Congress, "Religion and the Founding of the American Republic." Available at: www.loc.gov/exhibits/religion/rel02.html (accessed January 23, 2011).

10. James H. Hutson, ed., *Religion and the New Republic: Faith in the Founding of America* (Lanham, MD: Rowman & Littlefield Publishers Inc., 2000).

11. Alexis de Tocqueville, *Democracy in America*, Bruce Frohnen, ed. (Washington, D.C.: Regnery Publishing, Inc., 2002), 245.

12. Ibid., 33.

13. Deutsche, "French Headscarf Ban Not Discrimination, Says European Court," *The Muslim News Online*, February 27, 2009, www.muslimnews.co.uk/news/news.php?article=15819 (accessed January 25, 2011).

14. A. Stepan, *Arguing Comparative Politics* (New York: Oxford University Press, 2001), 213.

15. Robert Keohane, "The Globalization of Informal Violence, Theories of World Politics, and the 'Liberalism of Fear,'" *International Organization* (Spring, 2002), 29–43.

16. Interview of Madeline Albright with Bob Abernathy for PBS, "Madeline Albright: The Intersection of Religion and Foreign Policy," May 19, 2006. Also see "Madeline Albright, the Cardinal?" by Peter Steinfels, *The New York Times* (May 6, 2006).

17. Peter Berger and Thomas Lucker, *The Social Construction of Reality* (Garden City, NY: Anchor Books, 1967).

18. Peter Berger, interview article appeared in *The Christian Century*, October 29, 1997, 972–8.

19. Jonathan Fox, "Ethnoreligious Conflict in the Third World: The Role of Religion as a Cause of Conflict," *Nationalism and Ethnic Politics*, vol. 9, no. 1 (2003), 101–25.

20. Mark Lilla, "The Politics of God," *New York Times Magazine*, August 19, 2007. Available at: www.nytimes.com/2007/08/19/magazine/19Religion-t.html?_r=2&adxnnl=0&adxnnlx (accessed January 24, 2011).

21. Will Kymlicka, "Introduction: An Emerging Consensus?" *Ethical Theory and Moral Practice*, vol. 1, no. 2, (June, 1998), 143–57. Available at: http://0-www.jstor.org.library.lausys.georgetown.edu/stable/27504025 (accessed January 25, 2011); Abdullahi A. An-Na'im, "Synergy and Interdependence of Religion, Human Rights and Secularism," *Polylog: Forum for Intercultural Philosophy* (2001). Available at: www.polylog.org/them/2/fcs7-en.htm (accessed January 25, 2011).

22. Ibid.; also see "Racial and National Apartheid in Scripture" (Transvaal synod, 1948).

23. Madeleine Albright, *The Mighty and the Almighty* (New York: HarperCollins, 2006), 75.

24. U.S. Department of State, "Subject Index." Available at: www.state.gov/r/pa/ei/subject/index.htm (accessed January 25, 2011).

25. The three new courses are cited in Douglas Johnston, *Religion, Error, and Terror: U.S. Foreign Policy and the Challenge of Spiritual Engagement* (Santa Barbara, CA: Praeger, 2011), 92. The other observations are my own.

26. "Engaging Religious Communities Abroad" by Chicago Council Task Force.

27. I gratefully acknowledge Constitutional law scholar Kent Greenawalt for this formulation in a lengthy phone conversation; however, the position taken in this paragraph is my own and does not necessarily reflect his position, or his vast scholarship on First Amendment issues. See his two-volume *Religion and the Constitution* (Princeton, NJ: Princeton University Press, 2006, 2009).

28. *Hein v. Freedom From Religion Foundation*, 127 S. Ct. 2553, 2566–2568. A superb, comprehensive analysis of this can be found in Michael Kessler, "Does the

Establishment Clause Constrain Presidential Foreign Affairs Powers?" (unpublished manuscript, 2011).

29. Quoted in Robert Ruby and Timothy Samuel Shah, "Nigeria's Presidential Election: The Christian-Muslim Divide," *The Pew Forum on Religion & Public Life* (March 21, 2007), 143–58.

Chapter 4

1. www.catholicnewsagency.com/news/hillary_clinton_leaves_flowers_for_our_lady_of_guadalupe_asks_who_painted_it/ (accessed January 16, 2011).

2. Michael Lind, "For Liberal Internationalism," *The Nation* (June, 2007). Available at: www.thenation.com/doc/20070702/lind. A lengthier exposition of liberal internationalism, and how it is distinct from pacifist and other forms of liberalism in international affairs is Michael W. Doyle's essay "Liberalism Internationalism: War, Peace, and Democracy" (2004), available at the homepage of the Nobel Prize organization: http://nobelprize.org/nobel_prizes/peace/articles/doyle/index.html. This is a condensed argument from his prize-winning book, *Ways of War and Peace* (Oxford: Oxford University Press, 1997).

3. See the remarks by the Sultan of Sokoto, along with those of former U.S. ambassadors Princeton Lyman and John Campbell, on the importance of religious authority in Nigeria: "Islam and Democracy in Nigeria" [Rush Transcript, Federal News Service]. Event at the Council on Foreign Relations, November 19, 2007. Available at www.cfr.org/publication/14874/islam_and_democracy_in_nigeria_rush_transcript_federal_news_service.html (accessed November 22, 2010).

4. The story of the Iraq Inter-Religious Congress, initiated by Anglican Canon Bryan White and supported by the U.S. Department of Defense and other actors, was the third pillar of the 2007 strategy (including the "surge" and Sunni "Awakening") that turned around the disintegrating security situation in Iraq. See the Berkley Center Case Study, "Iraq: The Inter-Religious Congress for Peace and Security."

5. In recent years such analyses are beginning in the social sciences, but have not permeated the foreign policy apparatus. See for instance Jeffrey Haynes, "Transnational Religious Actors and International Politics," *Third World Quarterly I*, vol. 22, no. 2 (2001), 143–58.

6. Taken directly from *Foreign Policy* online, July 2007, www.foreignpolicy.com/story/cms.php?story_id=3906 (accessed October 13, 2010).

7. Remarks on a Human Rights Agenda for the Twenty-First Century, Secretary of State Hillary Clinton at Georgetown University, December 14, 2009. Available at: www.state.gov/secretary/rm/2009a/12/133544.htm (accessed September 8, 2010).

8. A recent study in the journal *Foreign Policy Analysis* reviews three types of economic statecraft to promote democracy: "top-down" (incentive to elites, such as Millennium Challenge Accounts), "bottom-up" (civil society and election support), and "inside" (technical and financial support to institutions, that is, legislatures, judiciaries, law enforcement). The reports surveyed in the article suggest that *ex ante* conditional "top down" programs, long-term "bottom-up" support to NGOs, journalists, activists, political parties, and elections (such as occurs through the National Endowment for Democracy [NED]), as pursued by the Reagan, Bush, and Clinton Administrations, are most likely to ultimately nurture and reinforce democratic transitions. However, institution-building programs typically fail to have long-term impact, and may even increase corruption. See Stephen D. Collins, "Can the U.S. Finance Freedom? Assessing U.S. Democracy Promotion Via Economic Statecraft," *Foreign Policy Analysis*, vol. 5, no. 4 (October, 2009), 384.

9. Arthur Schlesinger Jr. "Forgetting Reinhold Niebuhr, *The New York Times*, published September 18, 2005, http://www.nytimes.com/2005/09/18/books/review/18schlesinger.html (accessed May 18, 2011).

10. Eric D. Patterson, ed., *Christianity and Power Politics Today: Christian Realism and Contemporary Political Dilemmas* (New York: Palgrave Macmillan, 2008), 13.

11. Patterson, *Christianity and Power Politics Today*, 13.

12. Kenneth N. Waltz, *A Theory of International Politics* (New York: McGraw Hill, Inc., 1979); Michael W. Doyle, *Ways of War and Peace: Realism, Liberalism, and Socialism* (New York: Norton, 1997); Matthew Rendall, "Defensive Realism and the Concert of Europe," *Review of International Studies*, vol. 32, no. 3 (July, 2006), 523–40; Glenn H. Snyder, "Mearsheimer's World—Offensive Realism and the Struggle for Security: A Review Essay," *International Security*, vol. 27, no. 1 (2002), 149–73. Posted Online March 29, 2006 (doi:10.1162/016228802320 231253).

13. George Weigel, *Witness to Hope: the Biography of Pope John Paul II* (New York: HarperCollins, 1999).

14. United States Government: The White House, "National Security Strategy." Available at: www.whitehouse.gov/issues/homeland-security/ (accessed January 18, 2011).

15. Johnston, *Religion, Error, and Terror*, 7.

16. Thucydides, *Melian Dialogue*, published fifth century BCE; Hayward R. Alker, Jr, "The Dialectical Logic of Thucydides' Melian Dialogue," *The American Political Science Review*, vol. 82, no. 3 (September, 1988), 805–20.

17. Niccolo Machiavelli, *The Prince*, originally published 1516 (New York: Penguin Classics, 1971).

18. Alexander Wendt, "Anarchy is What States Make of It: The Social Construction of Power Politics," *International Organization*, vol. 46 (1992), 391–425 (doi:10.1017/S0020818300027764).

Chapter 5

1. Cristina Rojas and Judy Meltzer, eds, *Elusive Peace: International, National, and Local Dimensions of Conflict in Colombia* (New York: Palgrave Macmillan, 2005); Virginia M. Bouvier, ed., *Colombia: Building Peace in a Time of War* (Washington, D.C.: United States Institute of Peace Press, 2009).
2. Kenneth N. Waltz, *Man the State and War: A Theoretical Analysis* (New York: Columbia University Press, 1959).
3. Thomas Hobbes, *Leviathan: Or the Matter, Forme, and Power of a Common-Wealth Ecclesiasticall and Civill*, Ian Shapiro, ed. (New Haven, CT: Yale University Press, 2010).
4. David R. Mandel, "Instigators of Genocide: Examining Hitler from a Social Psychological Perspective," in L. S. Newman and R. Erber, eds, *Understanding Genocide: The Social Psychology of the Holocaust* (New York: Oxford University Press, 2002), 259–84. See also, Donald R. Ferrell, "The Unmourned Wound: Reflections on the Psychology of Adolf Hitler," *Journal of Religion and Health*, vol. 34, no. 3 (Fall, 1995), 175–97, published by Springer Article Stable URL: http://0-www.jstor.org.library.lausys.georgetown.edu/stable/27510921
5. Waltz, *Man the State and War*.
6. Dong Sun Lee, *Power Shifts, Strategy, and War: Declining States and International Conflict* (New York: Routledge, 2007), 114.
7. William Ben Hunt, *Getting to War: Predicting International Conflict with Mass Media Indicators* (Ann Arbor, MI: University of Michigan Press, 1997), 266.
8. Bassam Tibi, *Islam's Predicament with Modernity: Religious Reform and Cultural Change* (New York: Routledge, 2009), 9. Also see Tibi's "Inter-civilizational Conflict between Value Systems and Concepts of Order: Exploring the Islamic Humanist Potential for a Peace of Ideas," in Eric Patterson and John P. Gallagher, eds, *Debating the War of Ideas* (New York: Palgrave Macmillan, 2009), 157–73.
9. http://news.bbc.co.uk/1/hi/programmes/newsnight/5124762.stm and www.timesonline.co.uk/tol/news/world/article680339.ece (accessed December 30, 2010).
10. www.timesonline.co.uk/tol/news/world/article680339.ece (accessed December 17, 2010).
11. "Uganda: Religiously Inspired Insurgency," Berkley Center for Religion, Peace, & World Affairs. Available at: http://repository.berkleycenter.georgetown.edu/UgandaConflictCaseStudy.pdf (accessed January 16, 2011). See also, Tim Allen, *Trial Justice: The International Criminal Court and the Lord's Resistance Army* (New York: Zed Books, 2006). See also, Susanne Buckley-Zistel, *Conflict Transformation and Social Change in Uganda: Remembering after Violence* (New York: Palgrave Macmillan, 2008). See also, Donald H. Dunson, *Child, Victim, Soldier: The Loss of Innocence in Uganda* (New York: Orbis Books, 2008).
12. Suzanne J. Murdico, *Middle East Leaders: Osama bin Laden* (New York: The Rosen Publishing Group, Inc., 2007), 60.

13. R. Scott Appleby, *The Ambivalence of the Sacred: Religion, Violence, and Reconciliation* (Lanham, MD: Rowman & Littlefield Publishers, Inc., 2000).

14. "Report of the Liberhan Ayodhya Commission of Inquiry," published November 24, 2009, http://beta.thehindu.com/multimedia/archive/00014/Full_text_of_Liberha_14061a.pdf (accessed December 11, 2010, 23).

15. Hans Bakker, "Ayodhyā: A Hindu Jerusalem: An Investigation of 'Holy War' as a Religious Idea in the Light of Communal Unrest in India," *Numen*, vol. 38 (1991), 99.

16. "Ayodhya Verdict: Indian Holy Site 'to Be Divided'," BBC News. September 30, 2010.

17. Philip Jenkins, interview with the Carnegie Council's Public Affairs Program (April 17, 2002). Available at: www.carnegiecouncil.org/resources/transcripts/136.html (accessed January 19, 2011).

18. Brian Lennon, *After the Ceasefires: Catholics and the Future of Northern Ireland*, first edition (Dublin: Columbia Press, 1995). See also, David McKittrick and David McVea, *Making Sense of the Troubles: The Story of the Conflict in Northern Ireland* (Chicago, IL: New Amsterdam Books, 2002).

19. This data can be found in Hacic-Vlahovic, Ana, "(De)Secularization in Bosnia-Herzegovina: An Examination of Religiosity Trends in a Multi-Ethnic Society," *Amsterdam Social Science*, vol. 1, no. 1 (2008), 72–86.

20. Mitja Velikonja, *Religious Separation and Political Intolerance in Bosnia-Herzegovina* (College Station, TX: Texas A&M University Press, 2003) 240–1.

21. See Matthew 5.38–9.

22. John Paul Lederach and Paul Wehr, "Mediating Conflict in Central America," *Journal of Peace Research*, vol. 28, no. 1 (1991), 85–98 (doi: 10.1177/0022343391028001009) (accessed January 17, 2011). See also, Cynthia Sampson and John Paul Lederach, *From the Group Up: Mennonite Contributions to International Peacebuilding* (New York: Oxford University Press, 2000).

23. Anne Le Mare and Felicity McCartney, *Coming from the Silence: Quaker Peacebuilding Initiatives in Northern Ireland 1969–2007* (York, UK: William Sessions Ltd., 2009).

24. "Mozambique: Religious Peacebuilders Broker End to Civil War," Berkley Center for Religion, Peace, & World Affairs. Available at: http://repository.berkleycenter.georgetown.edu/010210MozambiqueCaseStudy.pdf (accessed January 17, 2011). See also, Jessica Schafer, *Soldiers at Peace: Veterans of the Civil War in Mozambique* (Hampshire: Palgrave Macmillan, 2007). See also, Christopher Alden, *Mozambique and the Construction of the New African State* (Basingstoke: Palgrave, 2001). See also, William Finnegan, *A Complicated War: The Harrowing of Mozambique* (Berkeley: University of California Press, 1993).

25. It should be noted that Tutu's views changed over time and that, not dissimilar to Reinhold Niebuhr and 1930s-era Christian realists, Tutu evolved from a position of nonviolence to apparently tacitly supporting a violent alternative if the

structural violence of apartheid were not to end. However, it is clear that he did not plan to participate in such a struggle, however justified it may have been.

26. Scott Appleby coined this term in his *The Ambivalence of the Sacred: Religion, Violence, and Reconciliation.* He applies "religious militancy" both to faith-inspired perpetrators of violence and to intense, faith-inspired action against violence.

27. Liberia's civil wars by George Klay Kieh Jr., in "Religious Leaders, Peacemaking, and the First Liberian Civil War," *Journal of Religion, Conflict, and Peace*, vol. 2, no. 2 (Spring, 2009), 1–15.

28. Stephen Ellis, *The Mask of Anarchy: The Destruction of Liberia and the Religious Dimension of an African Civil War* (New York: New York University Press, 2001). Veronica Fuest, "This is the Time to Get in Front: Changing Roles and Opportunities for Women in Liberia," *African Affairs*, vol. 107, no. 427 (2008), 201–24.

29. *Pray the Devil Back to Hell*, DVD. Abigail Disney, director, Fork Films, Llc, 2008. Republic of Liberia Truth and Reconciliation Commission. *Final Report: Volume II.* July 1, 2009. Available at www.trcofliberia.org/reports/final/final-report/trc-of-liberia-final-report-volume-ii.pdf (accessed September 27, 2010).

30. African Women and Peace Support Group, *Liberian Women Peacemakers: Fights for the Right be Seen, Heart and Counted* (Trenton, NJ: Africa World Press, Inc., 2004).

31. Gregory S. Gordon, "Complementarity and Alternative Justice," *Oregon Law Review*, vol. 88, no. 3 (2009), 621–702; For an introduction to Muslim avenues for reconciliation, see Eric Patterson, "Bury the Bloody Hatchet: Secularism, Islam, and Reconciliation in Afghanistan," *Journal of Interreligious Dialogue* no. 5 (Fall, 2010), 1–9.

32. Khaled Abou El Fadl, "Conflict Resolution as a Normative Value in Islamic Law: Handling Disputes with Non-Muslims," in Douglas Johnson, ed., *Faith-Based Diplomacy: Trumping Realpolitik* (Oxford: Oxford University Press, 2003), 194–5.

33. Sulayman Nyang and Douglas Johnston, "Conflict Resolution as a Normative Value in Islamic Law: Application to the Republic of Sudan," in Douglas Johnson, ed., *Faith-Based Diplomacy: Trumping Realpolitik* (Oxford: Oxford University Press, 2003), 220.

34. El Fadl, "Conflict Resolution as a Normative Value," 185.

35. Quoted in ibid., 184.

36. Ibid.

Chapter 6

1. Edward Perkins w/ Connie Cronley, *Mr. Ambassador: Warrior for Peace* (Norman: University of Oklahoma Press, 2000).

2. For a recent, best-selling description, see Walter Russell Mead's *Special Providence: American Foreign Policy and How It Changed the World* (New York: Routledge, 2002).

3. Albright, *The Mighty and the Almighty*, 75–6.

4. Johnston, *Religion, Error, and Terror*, 83.

5. Prothero, *Religious Literacy*, 11–12.

6. White House Press Statement on announcing Office of Faith-Based and Neighborhood Partnerships, February 5, 2009.

7. These guidelines are closely modeled on the "Lemon Test" criteria governing state interaction with some religious issues in the United States: must have a secular legislative purpose, must not have the primary effect of either advancing or inhibiting religion, nor result in an "excessive government entanglement" with religion. *Lemon v. Kurtzman*, 403 U.S. 602 (1971).

8. See www.usip.org/pubs/index.html (accessed August 30, 2010).

9. Speech given by Secretary of Defense Robert M. Gates at American University, April 14, 2008.

10. Quoted in Chaplain (LTC) Scottie Lloyd (USA), "Chaplain Contact with Local Religious Leaders: A Strategic Support," USAWC Strategy Research Project. Available at www.dtic.mil/cgi-bin/GetTRDoc?AD=ADA432751&Location=U2&doc=GetTRDoc.pdf (accessed January 7, 2011).

11. http://chaplain.ng.mil/Docs/Documents/jp1_05.pdf (accessed January 13, 2011).

12. Thomas F. Farr has repeatedly called for the former, as in his *World of Faith and Freedom: Why International Religious Liberty is Vital to American National Security* (New York: Oxford University Press, 2008). Douglas Johnston coined the term "religious attaché," in his *Faith-based Diplomacy: Trumping Realpolitik* (1997).

13. "Working with Faith-Based Organizations to Strengthen Human Resources for Health." Available at the USAID website, www.usaid.gov/pdf_docs/PNADJ074.pdf (accessed February 2, 2011).

14. Testimony before the House Committee on Foreign Affairs, Subcommittee on International Organizations, Human Rights, and Oversight by Dr. Steven Kull, Director, Program on International Policy Attitudes (PIPA), University of Maryland. Dr. Kull is Editor of WorldPublicOpinion.org and all data is available at that website. Testimony available at www.worldpublicopinion.org/pipa/articles/brmiddleeastnafricara/361.php?nid=&id=&pnt=361&lb=btvoc (accessed December 5, 2010). Also see John Esposito and Dalia Mogahed, *Who Speaks for Islam? What a Billion Muslims Really Think* (Washington, D.C.: Gallup Press, 2008).

15. Imam Feisal Abdul Rauf, *What's Right with Islam Is What's Right with America* (New York: HarperOne, 2006); Akbar Ahmed, *Journey Into America: The Challenge of Islam* (Washington, D.C.: Brookings Institution Press, 2010).

16. The tenth anniversary of IRFA becoming law was marked with a series of activities, including a special issue of the journal *Review of Faith and International Affairs*, the publication of a book on U.S. foreign policy and religious liberty by the former director of the State Department's Office of International Religious Freedom ("World of Faith and Freedom," Oxford University Press, 2008), and three symposia on IRFA hosted by Georgetown University and summarized in a program report titled "Georgetown Symposia on International Religious Freedom" and a separate policy recommendations brief titled *The Future of U.S. International Religious Freedom Policy*. The latter are available at http://berkleycenter.georgetown.edu/publications/977 and http://berkleycenter.georgetown.edu/publications/940 (accessed March 3, 2011).

17. William Jefferson Clinton in Madeleine Albright's *The Mighty and the Almighty*, x.

18. "USAID, Telling our Story: Strengthening Democracy in Mozambique," available at www.usaid.gov/stories/mozambique/ss_mozambique_election.html; "USAID, Telling our Story: Forestry Law Built on Consensus," available at www.usaid.gov/stories/philippines/ss_ph_forestry.html (accessed February 6, 2011).

Chapter 7

1. "Clerics Demand Death for Christian Convert," Associated Press, March 23, 2006.

2. "Clerics Call for Christian Convert's Death despite Western Outrage," Associated Press, March 23, 2006.

3. Jeremy Bentham, *Anarchical Follies*, quoted in N. Kinsella, "Tomorrow's Rights in the Mirror of History," in G. Gall, ed., *Civil Liberties in Canada* (Toronto: Butterworths, 1982), 17.

4. The history of human rights advocacy in this period is best chronicled in A. Hertzke, *Freeing God's Children: The Unlikely Alliance for Global Human Rights* (Lanham, MD: Rowman and Littlefield, 2004).

5. Edward Perkins w/ Connie Cronley, *Mr. Ambassador: Warrior for Peace*.

6. Secretary of State Hillary Rodham Clinton, quoted in "Clinton Reiterates U.S. Commitment to 'Robust' Rights Agenda," in *The Washington Post*, March 12, 2009, A14.

7. Barack Obama at Compassion Forum (April 13, 2008).

8. At first this advocacy resulted in a joint statement in late 1996 by the House and Senate, "Condemning the Persecution of Christians Worldwide." During 1995–1998 numerous meetings on the issues surrounding religious liberty and religious persecution were conducted in Washington, D.C., and the U.S. Department of State published the findings and recommendations of a new Advisory Committee on International Religious Freedom. During that time a hard-fought battle was joined between supporters and opponents of legislation

that would explicitly commit the U.S. government to promote religious freedom worldwide. A key issue was whether making international religious freedom an overt part of U.S. foreign policy would tie the hands of the White House and State Department in diplomatic affairs. Another cluster of issues surrounded the content and expectations of the legislation itself: should the work of new U.S. government institutions on religious freedom be informative, punitive, or something else in their nature and recommendations?

9. The tenth anniversary of IRFA becoming law was marked with a series of activities, including a special issue of the journal *Review of Faith and International Affairs*, the publication of a book on U.S. foreign policy and religious liberty by the former director of the State Department's Office of International Religious Freedom, and three symposia on IRFA hosted by Georgetown University and synthesized into a policy recommendations brief for the Obama Administration titled, *The Future of U.S. International Religious Freedom Policy.*

10. "U.S. Lodges Strong Protest in Vietnam," in *Catholic News Agency Online*, January 8, 2011. Available at: www.catholicnewsagency.com/news/us-lodges-strong-protest-with-vietnam-after-beating-of-american-diplomat/ (accessed February 5, 2011).

11. Briefing by Brian J. Grim, a senior researcher at the Pew Research Center's Forum on Religion & Public Life, was presented to the Foreign Affairs Subcommittee on International Organizations, Human Rights, and Oversight on the Pew Forum's findings on restrictions on religion around the world, March 19, 2010. Available at: http://pewforum.org/Government/Briefing-on-US-International-Religious-Freedom-Policy.aspx (accessed February 1, 2011).

12. Jennifer Windsor, "Advancing the Freedom Agenda: Time for a Recalibration?" *The Washington Quarterly*, vol. 29, no. 3 (Summer, 2006), 32.

13. Amy Zegart, "The Legend of a Democracy Promoter," *The National Interest Online*, September 16, 2008. Available at www.nationalinterest.org/Article.aspx?id=19688 (accessed February 2, 2011).

14. The transcript of this address is available at www.thechicagocouncil.org/dynamic_page.php?id=64 (accessed November 17, 2010).

15. "Remarks by the President on a New Beginning," June 4, 2009. Available at: www.whitehouse.gov/the-press-office/remarks-president-cairo-university-6-04-09 (accessed November 21, 2010).

16. William Jefferson Clinton in Madeleine Albright's *The Mighty and the Almighty*, x.

17. Condoleezza Rice, "Rethinking the National Interest: American Realism for a New World," *Foreign Affairs*, vol. 87, no. 4 (July/August, 2008), 2–26.

18. Correlations between the Hudson Institute's Religious Freedom Score and the other measures reported by Grim (2008) are all statistically significant at $p < 0.001$, two-tailed, and are as follows: Freedom House civil liberty index (0.862); Freedom House political liberty index (0.822); Reporters Without Borders press freedom index (0.804); Heritage Foundation economic freedom index (0.743); and the longevity of democracy index (0.646).

19. A new initiative studying spiritual capital is funded by the John Templeton Foundation (www.templeton.org/funding_areas/core_themes/spiritual_capital/); for papers offering an analysis of religion from a "religious economies" perspective, see www.religionomics.com/ (accessed March 12, 2011).

20. See Harold G. Koenig, Michael E. McCullough, and David B. Larson, *Handbook of Religion and Health* (New York: Oxford University Press, 2000).

21. See Eric M. Uslaner, "Religion and Civic Engagement in Canada and the United States," *Journal for the Scientific Study of Religion*, vol. 41, no. 2 (June, 2002), 239–54, and Corwin Smidt, "Religion and Civic Engagement: A Comparative Analysis," *Annals of the American Academy of Political and Social Science* 565 (September, 1999), 176–92.

22. Arthur Sullivan and Steven M. Sheffrin, *Economics: Principles in Action* (Upper Saddle River, NJ: Pearson-Prentice Hall, 2003), 471.

23. Rachel M. McCleary and Robert J. Barro, "Private Voluntary Organizations involved in International Development Assistance, 1939–2004," *Nonprofit and Voluntary Sector Quarterly*, vol. 37, no. 3 (2008), 512–36.

24. Farah Stockman, Michael Kranish, and Peter S. Canellos, Kevin Baron, "Bush Brings Faith to Foreign Aid," *The Boston Globe* (October 8, 2006).

25. Andrew Natsios, "Five Debates on International Development: The US Perspective," *Development Policy Review*, vol. 24, no. 2 (2006), 135.

26. Katherine Marshall and Marisa Van Saanen, *Development and Faith: Where Mind, Heart, and Soul Work Together* (Washington, D.C.: The World Bank, 2008).

27. Natsios, "Five Debates on International Development," 133.

28. Marshal and Van Saanen, *Development and Faith*, 155–6.

29. These guidelines are closely modeled on the "Lemon Test" criteria governing state interaction with some religious issues in the United States: must have a secular legislative purpose, must not have the primary effect of either advancing or inhibiting religion, nor result in an "excessive government entanglement" with religion (*Lemon v. Kurtzman*, 403 U.S. 602 (1971)).

30. This point is made by Jeffrey Haynes in his presentation, "Religion and Development: A General Introduction," Copenhagen, September 2008. Available at the World Bank's website.

Chapter 8

1. Rachel Bronson, *Thicker than Oil: America's Uneasy Partnership with Saudi Arabia* (New York: Oxford University Press, 2006).

2. Alexis de Tocqueville, *Democracy in America* (1831).

3. Pew Global Attitudes Survey (2007).

4. Gallup report cited in *The Washington Times* (March 3, 2009), A3.

5. The 2007 Religious Landscape Survey is available at: http://religions.pewforum.org/reports# (accessed January 16, 2011).

6. Alfred C. Stepan, "Religion, Democracy, and the 'Twin Tolerations,'" *Journal of Democracy*, vol. 11, no. 4 (October, 2000), 37–57.

7. Joseph Ghougassian, *The Knight and the Falcon: The Coming of Christianity in Qatar, A Muslim Nation* (Escondido, CA: Lukas and Son, 2008). This excerpt was originally written by me for the Chicago Council on Global Affairs' report *Engaging Religious Communities Abroad* (2010). It has been slightly modified for this chapter.

8. Both stories, and others, quoted in Chaplain (LTC) Scottie Lloyd (USA), "Chaplain Contact with Local Religious Leaders: A Strategic Support," USAWC Strategy Research Project, available at www.dtic.mil/cgi-bin/GetTRDoc?AD=A DA432751&Location=U2&doc=GetTRDoc.pdf

9. Source: Summary Report, 2006 by Robert Heffner.

10. Chris Seiple www.christianitytoday.com/ct/2007/may/25.30.html (accessed September 28, 2010).

11. www.icrd.org/storage/icrd/documents/salam_institute_evaluation_final.pdf (accessed November 15, 2010).

Index